START AND RUN A
Restaurant

START AND RUN A
Restaurant

Carol Godsmark

howtobooks / **smallbusinessstart-ups**

Published by How To Books Ltd,
Spring Hill House, Spring Hill Road,
Begbroke, Oxford OX5 1RX, United Kingdom
Tel: (01865) 375794, Fax: (01865) 379162
info@howtobooks.co.uk
www.howtobooks.co.uk

First edition 2005
Reprinted 2005
Reprinted 2006
Reprinted 2008
Second edition 2010

British Library Cataloguing in Publication Data
A catalogue record for this book is available from the British Library

ISBN 978 1 84528 390 2

Produced for How To Books by Deer Park Productions, Tavistock, Devon
Typeset by Pantek Arts Ltd, Maidstone, Kent
Printed and bound in Great Britain by Cromwell Press Group, Trowbridge, Wiltshire

CONTENTS

Acknowledgements   ix
Foreword   xi
Preface   xv

1. Running your own restaurant   **1**
    ☐ Why run your own restaurant?   1
    ☐ How suitable are you?   1
    ☐ Seeing yourself as a restaurateur   3

2. Choosing your Restaurant   **5**
    ☐ Deciding what kind of restaurant   5
    ☐ New trends in restaurants   6

3. Location, Design and Legal Requirements   **8**
    ☐ Location, Location, Location   9
    ☐ Spotting current trends   10
    ☐ Taking the first steps on the property ladder 11
    ☐ Franchising a business   14
    ☐ Local government and your business   14
    ☐ Scrutinising a property   15
    ☐ Kitchen layout   15
    ☐ First impressions   20
    ☐ Licences   20
    ☐ Music   22
    ☐ Smoking   22
    ☐ Complying with Acts   23
    ☐ Price Marking (Food and Drink on Premises)
      Order 2003   26
    ☐ Your checklist   27

4. Financing your Business   **28**
    ☐ Creating income   28
    ☐ A business plan   29
    ☐ Forming a company   30
    ☐ Calculating menu costings and prices   31
    ☐ Tipping   36
    ☐ Attracting finance   36
    ☐ Raising capital and obtaining business partners/investors 37

☐ Working in a partnership   38
☐ Capital expenditure   38
☐ Next steps in finding funding   40
☐ Value Added Tax (VAT)   42
☐ Payroll   44
☐ Insurance   44
☐ Credit cards   47
☐ Legal tips   47
☐ Business advice organisations   48

5. Running a Safe Business   50
☐ Food safety regulations   50
☐ Storing food   51
☐ Food poisoning and avoiding contamination   52
☐ Staff hygiene   55
☐ Environmental health   55

6. Choosing the Design and Equipment   59
☐ Designing your restaurant   59
☐ Is your restaurant functional?   60
☐ The hall and bar   61
☐ Laying out the restaurant   62
☐ Laying out the kitchen   68
☐ Buying china and tableware   75
☐ Organising the service   78

7. Marketing your Business   80
☐ Finding your target market   81
☐ Choosing your restaurant's name   81
☐ Signage   82
☐ Promotional material   83
☐ Advertising   86
☐ Creating your media profile   90
☐ Dealing with critics   93
☐ The guides   95
☐ Expanding your business   100

8. Staffing the Well Run Restaurant   108
☐ The importance of service   109
☐ Finding staff   110
☐ Motivating your staff   112

☐ Getting off to a good start 113
☐ Other employment tips 116
☐ Employing people 118
☐ Kitchen hierachy terminology 123
☐ The kitchen career 125
☐ Teamworking 126
☐ Dress code, behaviour and communicating
with customers 126
☐ Management skills 130
☐ Staff rotas 131

9. Designing Menus **134**
☐ The importance of the menu 134
☐ Food consistency 134
☐ Creating a menu 135
☐ Using first-rate produce 137
☐ What to cook and why to cook it 137
☐ Menu and drink pricing 140
☐ Creating contented customers 140
☐ Writing and compiling the menu 142
☐ Accommodating special diets 147
☐ Instructing your kitchen staff on following your recipes 148

10. Choosing Suppliers **151**
☐ Looking for key suppliers 151
☐ Working with your suppliers 151
☐ Sourcing locally 152
☐ Sourcing alternatives 154
☐ Quality and provenance of produce 156
☐ Useful contacts for sourcing produce 157

11. Organising Wine and Other Drinks **160**
☐ Getting wines right 160
☐ The diverse wine list 161
☐ Wine and food 165
☐ Pricing wine 167
☐ Wine vocabulary 167
☐ Water, coffee and tea 169
☐ Trading Standards guidelines for selling alcohol 170

12. Running your Restaurant on a day-to-day basis   173
☐ Planning   173
☐ Preparation   173
☐ Division of labour   174
☐ Cleaning up   174
☐ Front of house   175
☐ The kitchen   179
☐ A typical day at Soanes Restaurant   179
☐ Why do it?   182

13. Customer Relations and Being a Customer   183
☐ Customer satisfaction   183
☐ Handling complaints   184
☐ Promoting customer satisfaction   185
☐ Being a customer   188

Postscript   189

Glossary   190

Useful Contacts   193

Bibliography   195

Index   196

ACKNOWLEDGEMENTS

Researching this book has unearthed many enthusiastic, dedicated professional people who have generously contributed their time and expertise and whom I thank most sincerely:

Peter Gordon of Providores, London; Kit Chapman, the Castle Hotel, Taunton, Somerset, and Brazz Restaurants; Jonathan Cooper, Amano Cafe, London; Jake Watkins, JSW, Petersfield, Hampshire; Raymond Blanc and Tracey Clinton, Manoir Aux Quat' Saisons; Laurence Murphy, Fat Olives; Ray Farthing, 36 On The Quay; Chris Allwood, Allwood's Wine Bar; Alistair Gibson, Brookfield Hotel; all of Emsworth, Hampshire; Larry Stone, wine director, Rubicon, San Francisco, California; John Hayler, Planning Department, Chichester District Council; Lawrence Foord and Sarah Parker, Trading Standards, CDC; John White, Environmental Protection, CDC; David Knowles-Ley, Environmental Health, CDC; Julian Mitchell, Christie & Co, London; Brian Duckett and Paul Monaghan, Howarth Franchising, London; Lorna and Peter Walters, solicitors, Streathers, London; Andrew Turvil, Editor of *The Good Food Guide* and the *Which? Pub Guide*; Emma Rickett, the AA; Frances Gill, *Harden's Guides*; Paul Cordle, *The Michelin Guide of Great Britain and Ireland*; Alex Chambers, *Les Routiers Guide*; Soraya Conway, *Zagat Survey*; Sarah Guy, *Time Out Guides*; Georgina Campbell's *Jameson Guide – Ireland*; Julian Shaw, Small Business Service statistics; Joanna Wood, *Caterer and Hotelkeeper*; Simon Henrick, Brake catering; Elizabeth Crompton-Batt, Charles Secrett, Mark Haynes and staunch friends and allies Anna Fleming, Chrissie Bates, Jocelyn and Peter Sampson, Noel Ross-Russell, Caroline Godsmark, Ruth Carver and others who have shown much patience, goodwill, encouragement and understanding including Louise, Jackie, Rennie and Gary Reynolds and Guild of Food Writers co-members.

FOREWORD

Owning and running a restaurant will be, I guarantee, the most exhausting, nerve-wracking and tiring thing you will ever do. If it goes well it will also be the most satisfying and rewarding part of your life – much like raising children. Carol has clearly laid out all the pitfalls you will encounter and the strategies you need to have in place, and if you read this book cover to cover well before you embark on a life as a restaurateur you will be rewarded with foresight. It's a hard life and it can be a great life – but get prepared. Read this book.

Peter Gordon

To Jonathan, Matthew and Caroline who lived the restaurant
life to the full

PREFACE

Are you passionate about restaurants? Do you hanker after opening your own restaurant? If so, you would be entering a very buoyant market because more people are choosing to eat out than ever before. There are over 263,000 outlets selling food, including hotels, restaurants, fast-food outlets, pubs and other forms of the leisure industry. Despite the recession, the industry is still buoyant. Eating out is one of the UK's formost social activities and constitutes about one third of what is spent on food.

This increase in the numbers of people eating out is due, in part, to the structure of households. We are a cash-rich, time-poor society that prefers to meet up with friends and family in restaurants rather than to slave over a hot stove at home.

Thanks to the wide range of restaurants offering a great variety of food to suit every budget, singles, families and older couples now eat out on a regular basis. One in three of us eats out once a week or more. The customer is now more discerning and is able to demand better quality, better prices, consistency and choice. Otherwise they vote with their feet.

Opening and running a restaurant is an aspiration many people have. They dream of ditching a dull job and entering a world of creativity and hospitality, of being their own boss. Or this may naively be seen as a money-for-old-rope venture, tossing a salad or turning a steak under a hot grill being about as taxing as the cooking gets. They may also think that customers will come through their door from day one without much effort on their part.

Restaurants are part of the hospitality and entertainment business, but this is a tough business. It is also a most rewarding, stimulating one, both on a personal and financial level if the business is approached and run with prudence, professionalism, control, dedication and a dash of imagination and flair. And you have to like people.

As a restaurant journalist, critic and chef (I am also a restaurant consultant, guide inspector and past restaurateur), I have researched and written *Start and Run a Restaurant* from practical experience. The chapters includes aspects of the restaurant trade from location and licence applications to finance and professional advice.

Start and Run a Restaurant also covers equipment, marketing, restaurant reviews, staffing, suppliers, menus, wines, the day-to-day running of the restaurant, complaints and how to deal with them, building up a loyal trade and – crucially – putting yourself in your customers' shoes.

The book is full of up-to-date information for the novice restaurateur. It also offers advice to those already in the business who may wish to trade up to meet current customer expectations. It includes useful trade addresses, an index and a whole host of top tips throughout the book based on the experiences of seasoned chefs, restaurateurs, suppliers and others in the profession whom I have interviewed for this book.

If your passion for running a restaurant takes hold, I wish you every success and fulfilment in one of the oldest, more rewarding trades in the world, the restaurant and hospitality trade.

1

RUNNING YOUR OWN RESTAURANT

Running a restaurant is a dream many people have. But turning that dream into reality can mean taking a frightening step into the unknown, especially if you are currently in a secure job. You need first to be very sure of why you want to go into the restaurant business and then you need to acquire as much knowledge of the business as you can.

WHY RUN YOUR OWN RESTAURANT?

If you are currently an employee you may feel that your work is unrewarding, dull and unpredictable, or you may be locked into a profession that no longer inspires you and you want to take control of your own destiny. Perhaps you are longing to develop your creative and business side and have always felt attracted to the idea of running your own restaurant.

If you are a very good cook and enjoy producing marvellous meals for friends and family, you may find the idea of doing it for a living a very exciting prospect. But you should be more than just a good cook to sustain the business week in week out. You, or your partner, also need to be a good front-of-house manager, to be able to manage staff, understand and even do the accounts, do the ordering and offer excellent hospitality to customers.

Whatever the motivating force behind you deciding to start and run your own restaurant, the good news is that more and more people are eating out. The result is a mushrooming of restaurants to suit every culinary whim. The bad news is that the business is not suited to everyone, despite any strong aspirations you may have. So the first thing you must do is to examine carefully whether running a resturant is the right business for you.

HOW SUITABLE ARE YOU?

First examine your strengths and your character – and the strengths and characters of those in partnership with you – by asking yourself these questions:

☐ Are you fed up with your job and looking for a change of lifestyle?

☐ Do you see yourself opening a restaurant in a beautiful area as part of a new, easier lifestyle?

☐ Do you want to be your own boss and so keep the profits?

☐ Are you really positive about creating a new business?

☐ Are you motivated, organised and self-disciplined?

☐ Have you taken on board the fact that you are saying goodbye to a secure pay packet and fringe benefits?

☐ Have you discussed with your family how this change in lifestyle will affect them?

☐ Because your busiest period will be the weekends, how will this tally with your family life?

☐ Are your family committed to this change of lifestyle and will they back you wholeheartedly?

☐ Do you like people? Have you the skills to deal with the idiosyncrasies of both customers and staff?

☐ Are you a good communicator?

☐ Are you prepared for what will perhaps be a long haul before your business is successful?

☐ Do you and your business partner(s) share the right temperaments for the hospitality business?

☐ Are you a problem-solver? A decision-maker?

☐ Are you confident enough to sell your business plan to banks, customers and the media?

☐ Can you take advice? Learn new skills?

☐ Can you delegate?

☐ Can you prioritise?

☐ How good are you at coping with stress?

☐ Do you have good health?

☐ Do you have a warm personality? A hospitable nature?

☐ Do you have the stamina to work long hours?

☐ Are you flexible? Calm? Reasonable? Positive?

☐ How do you *really* feel about the service industry?

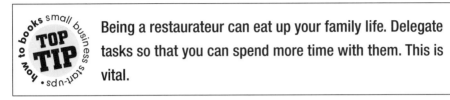

Being a restaurateur can eat up your family life. Delegate tasks so that you can spend more time with them. This is vital.

These questions should be answered honestly. It is a long list of searching questions, and you may never have been tested on some of these strengths, but you and those entering the business with you will need the majority of these strengths to run a successful resturant. If most of your answers are positive, you will achieve the other attributes along the way.

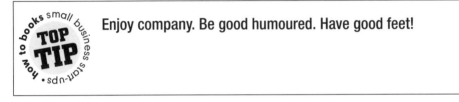

Enjoy company. Be good humoured. Have good feet!

SEEING YOURSELF AS A RESTAURATEUR

Think about what kind of a restaurateur you see yourself as. You might be someone who offers acceptable food and is in the business purely as a money-making venture. Or you could be a restaurateur who sees the trade as a way of life. You may be seeking to change, mature, explore new ideas and learn from other chefs and restaurateurs, but also, through judicious management, to stay afloat financially. Your restaurant will reflect your personality.

Being a restaurateur *is* a hard, unrelenting, competitive way of life but it can be hugely satisfying, rewarding, entertaining and stimulating. The people you work with are an immensely important factor in making this happen, as well as in creating an atmosphere for customers to relax in by offering good food that is thoughtfully and skilfully prepared.

Being a restaurateur requires creativity and passion, boundless energy, commitment and enthusiasm. Dispensing hospitality is the way of life you are choosing when deciding to run a restaurant. If this is not for you, then running a restuarant is not the right business for you.

Should you decide to join this way of life, you will be entering one of the oldest professions in the world, one that is very much part of life in all cultures. It is pure theatre.

2
CHOOSING YOUR RESTAURANT

Because the British public are eating out more and more often, the types and styles of restaurants have diversified to meet this demand. One in three of us are eating out at least once a week.

DECIDING WHAT KIND OF RESTAURANT

You might want to run a fast-food restaurant, a mid-range restaurant or a family-run café. Or perhaps a pasta/pizza eatery, a small restaurant in the town or country, or an upmarket restaurant with all the fripperies. Or will you be joining those who take on a pub, serving good, medium-priced food without all the extras?

Perhaps you lean towards a restaurant serving ethnic food, a daytime café or tearoom serving freshly made lunches and teas, a mainly fish restaurant or an informal café offering all manner of inexpensive food for the passing tourist trade.

As the restaurant trade is so diverse, you will have to do a lot of research. Is there a glut of pizza/pasta chain restaurants already in the neighbourhood? Or do you think you can offer even better pizza and pasta than those already on offer and still be priced competitively? Think of their buying power, advertising, big business backing and then think again.

Repeat business will be guaranteed if you've got the right feel and the right food, a good selection of wines by the glass and bottle, and decent on-tap local beers. And, it goes without saying, good, knowledgeable, friendly staff.

You will need to decide whether you will welcome children into your restaurant. In Britain children are largely seen as a nuisance, unlike our European cousins who tend to welcome children into their restaurants with open arms. Families with children are genuinely welcomed and given an ordinary table anywhere in the restaurant, not just in the back recesses.

 Encourage the children in your restaurant to eat all the types of food on offer. Children are the next generation of diners.

As Matthew Fort, a food journalist for the *Guardian Weekend* and former restaurant reviewer, noted on a visit to a hotel restaurant: 'It's hotel policy to ban children under the age of 12, a policy that I overheard being enthusiastically endorsed by a party at a nearby table. It sent me into a towering rage. How typically middle-aged, middle-class, blinkered, selfish and British. I can think of no justification for marginalising children in this way, particularly as, in my experience, they can often give their elders a lesson in manners.'

Hear, hear Matthew!

NEW TRENDS IN RESTAURANTS

New, good restaurants are cropping up throughout the UK. What is lacking are good neighbourhood restaurants for everyday eating as found in many other countries.

Delicatessens with restaurants

Delicatessens with attached restaurants are also on the increase and can open all day and evening or, depending on their location, only during the day to catch the business trade. They have cropped up in London, Bristol, Brighton, Chichester, Manchester and Totnes and in many other towns to great acclaim.

All-day cafés

Other trends include all-day cafés serving excellent breakfasts, elevenses (where else in the world except Britain?), brunches, light lunches and teas. They may also open in the evening as a more upmarket restaurant, maximising the potential of the space to cover the high costs of maintaining the site.

Following the trends

These trends may help to show you which route to take. Consider where you are based. Is there a passing trade? If so, you could offer good loose-leaf tea, the best coffee and a good range of simple, easily prepared dishes for those in a hurry. Also consider whether your customer will be shoppers or those on business in the area.

The New Zealand chef, Peter Gordon, well known for his fusion food, is a prime example of how to do this with style and simplicity. The Providores, the award-winning London restaurant he jointly owns with three partners, is a union of restaurant, all-day café, meeting place and wine bar.

The casual, professionally run place offers the lot – laksas, tortillas, soups, freshly baked breads, bowls of nuts and olives, sardines, soy-braised duck, New Zealand venison, smoothies, teas, coffees, freshly squeezed juices, etc. – in the downstairs

Tapa Room from 9 am to 10.30 pm. The Providores upstairs offers an equally eclectic mix of dishes on its constantly changing menu.

Beyond the big cities

Can this mix be achieved outside the large cities? West Sussex's Chichester has a similar restaurant. The Dining Room is a wine bar cum restaurant offering not only mezes but also Danish open sandwiches. Included on the menu are charcuterie and specially selected cheese plates, salads, starters, game, beef, lamb and fish main courses and omelettes. In short, the owners made a decision to appeal to a broad market, including pre-theatre diners. It works because they have researched their market and have responded to it.

Small, family-run restaurants with minimal seating and offering terrific authentic Middle-Eastern food are also proving to be immensely popular. The prices are low and the atmosphere, created by hookahs, low sofas and Arab music, makes these restaurants popular places to eat.

Know your market and to whom you are catering. Then design your premises, menu, pricing, service, etc.

3

LOCATION, DESIGN AND LEGAL REQUIREMENTS

Having narrowed down the area where you wish to run your business you must next decide whether to buy or rent a property. First you should contact commercial property estate agents who will offer you their considerable wealth of local knowledge. For example:

☐ What are the local trends in the restaurant trade?

☐ Will you need planning permission?

☐ How will you negotiate the property ladder?

You will also need to talk to environmental health officers about the required standards for running a restaurant.

This chapter deals with these subjects and also provides tips for scrutinising, buying and renting properties and for franchising and leases. It also deals with:

☐ local government issues;

☐ refuse collection;

☐ alcohol and public entertainment licences;

☐ fire regulations;

☐ access and facilities for the disabled;

☐ the Sale of Goods Act;

☐ the law concerning sex discrimination and the Race Relations Act;

☐ the Hotel Proprietor's Act;

☐ water supply and pest control;

☐ kitchen layout;

☐ ventilation; and

☐ music and smoking.

LOCATION, LOCATION, LOCATION

The popular conception for a truly successful restaurant is that the three Ls are sacrosanct. This may be true in a city because the customers are close by, whether they live, work or are staying in hotels near your restaurant. By contrast, some of the most successful restaurants are in remote areas. So how do they create a good, solid customer base? Thanks to the superb ingredients cooked to a high standard and the sheer beauty of the location, people will make the detour to a well run, perhaps seasonal, restaurant.

Compare the restaurant *Gordon Ramsay* in London's Chelsea, where you need to book months in advance, with the highly popular *The Three Chimneys* on the Isle of Skye, a 40-seater restaurant down a single track. One is about as remote as it gets in the British Isles, the other one of the most central. What really matters is how the business is run once the right location has been chosen.

Narrowing it down

You've decided on your area and are thinking of buying or renting a property. Visit it a number of times on different days and times of the day. This will give you a better flavour of the area, the type of people, the activity, and it will also give you a more informed view of the property. Does the lighting need improving, the decoration updating, the entrance made more welcoming and accessible?

If possible, sit for a time in the restaurants you have selected and imagine a business working in the building. Does it suit your plans? Is it enhanced by a view? Has it character? Are the proportions right?

Outline your plans to friends or those in the restaurant business and talk over the details with them. They may be able to throw light on a particular problem that has so far eluded you. Or they may give good advice as to why not to open such a restaurant in the area.

Put yourself in your customers' shoes. If there are competitors in the same area, are there too many of the same type of restaurant as yours? You may struggle for business unless you offer something different. But, equally, you may pick up overflow from successful nearby restaurants if the public see the area as a place for eating out.

There is usually a good reason for a gastronomic desert. Look at Guildford in Surrey. Very few good restaurants and nothing worth a mention in the *Good Food Guide*. Why? Easy commuting into London where many commuting residents prefer eating out is one explanation. Expensive property is another.

SPOTTING CURRENT TRENDS

Consumer education about food continues to increase thanks to travel abroad. The emphasis on food, drink, produce and hospitality in the media is also continuing at an unprecedented pace. So the question your customer might ask is 'why can't I get that here?'

Expectations are constantly rising. There are many price levels to choose from, as well as styles of cooking, restaurant design and atmosphere. Who would have thought basement premises could be sold as desirable places to eat in? Enter Wagamama, the successful slurping-noodle chain that established their restaurants in basements. Their style of fast, casual, good food has proved a runaway hit. But a word of warning: few other basement restaurants achieve this, or upstairs restaurants for that matter. People like to see the entire establishment at street level.

Some current trends to look out for are as follows:

☐ High inner-city rents, thanks to corporate businesses vying for hot property addresses and willing to pay over the odds for these, have meant that restaurateurs are now looking at the suburbs, smaller towns and the countryside for properties.

☐ Individual neighbourhood restaurants are making a comeback because of the public's disaffection with branded restaurants and pubs. They are now looking for a more personal approach.

☐ Due to drink-drive regulations and difficulties with parking, neighbourhood restaurants have the edge over their drive-to competitors.

☐ Conveyor-belt ethnic food – Japanese, Chinese, Thai, Indian – is gaining favour with younger people.

☐ Gastro pubs have become increasingly popular in London over the last 18 years and are making their mark on the rest of the UK and Ireland. There is more profit in quality food than in drink.

☐ Run-down pubs are popular premises to buy and turn into wine bars or cafés with the emphasis on bistro-type food.

☐ There has been a big resurgence in developing inner-city areas and former docklands, such as in Bristol, Liverpool and Newcastle, with restaurants opening up to fill demand.

☐ Small, simple, very casual, minimal-comfort combined deli-cafés are opening in cities to attract business customers during office hours and the early evening.

☐ Small niche restaurants are opening in medium-sized and large towns.

☐ Fast/casual restaurants are in great demand, not only by customers but also by venture capital investors.

☐ Contemporarily designed restaurants with clean lines, wooden floorboards, good lighting and music attract customers and will continue to do so, say the agents. Carpeted premises and not being able to see inside the premises from the street are big turnoffs.

☐ Twenty-four hour cafés are also possible now that that licensing laws have been extended.

☐ One in three Londoners eats out at least once a week. The rest of Britain may be behind this but changes in working/leisure patterns and a greying population who can afford to eat out may mean this trends spreads to the whole of the UK.

TAKING THE FIRST STEPS ON THE PROPERTY LADDER

First, find a solicitor who specialises in commercial property transactions for either renting or buying a property. Draw up a business plan and then have this approved by your bank.

If you are renting, prepare a good presentation pack to win the landlord's approval. Use some graphics to inject that wow factor, particularly if the property is in London as that is expected in the capital. Out-of-town presentations don't need to be as sophisticated, according to the commercial property agents.

Put in your presentation the anticipated covers, the spend per head, whether you intend to turn tables (i.e. the same table to be used several times at one sitting) and the proposed accounting.

Go through *Yellow Pages* or buy a catering magazine such as *Caterer and Hotelkeeper* to see who the agents are in your area. Good agents will get to know you, their client, instead of introducing you to masses of properties that don't suit your wishes. Be sure you make it clear to the agent what kind of property you are seeking. But be prepared to be flexible when viewing properties as you may be surprised at some property's potential.

First and foremost, however, you must understand your market. This should come first, before you enter into any contract and despite the excitement of falling in love with a property. Do you fit into this area? Who will your customers be?

Renting the property

If you are renting premises, measure the property yourself. The area could be less than that given by estate agents or landlords and the rent should therefore be lowered. Negotiate a lower rent if you are taking out a long lease. If the property needs repairs or major redecoration, ask for a rent-free period or discount until these are carried out.

Always obtain an agreement in writing for all dealings with landlords or estate agents, especially for any major alterations you would like to make to the property. Check on planning permission with your local council if you are putting up new signage or if there is a change of use of the property.

Buying leasehold or freehold

Find an architect whose practice deals in restaurant development. Ask them to visit the property with you to discuss any alterations you may like to make and be guided by their expertise. Instruct a solicitor to act for you.

Communication is vital between buyer and seller. Keep people up to speed.

Discuss with environmental health officers (EHOs) the basic requirements, such as hand basins for staff, refrigeration, kitchen extractors and fire extinguishers (see page 56 for a fuller view of the EHO's role and expectations).

Questions to ask

Before buying or renting an established restaurant, find the answers to the following questions:

☐ Is the area saturated with similar restaurants?

☐ Are the owners experiencing restaurant burnout or are there other reasons for the sale/change of lease?

☐ Is there a local development that will adversely affect the area? Or, conversely, will it add to customer potential?

☐ How old is the business and how long has it been profitable?

☐ What is the profit margin for the past few years?

☐ What percentage of repeat business is there?

☐ Do the books look accurate? Do the assets outweigh the liabilities? (Ask your solicitor's or finance consultant's advice.)

☐ Have all the renovations been undertaken with the necessary approval?

Leases: a brief guide

The average leasehold lease is 25 years with other leases at 20 or 15 years, but these can be negotiated with the landlord. A freehold lease's finance changes only with the cost of borrowing.

☐ Landlords are looking for long-term investments and so, if the tenant has no track record, the landlord may ask for a year's rent deposit in advance or a bank guarantee.

☐ However, the tenant may ask for a rent-free period if money is being spent on the property, such as for rewiring, redecorating or new plumbing.

☐ The lease should be a full-repairing and insuring one with five-year rent reviews – the rent only increasing, never decreasing.

☐ The amount of the rent increase may be calculated on profits or a comparable method of calculation.

☐ A break clause is advisable. This is a walk-away sum should the lease be broken.

☐ A sub-let clause should also be included.

☐ It is, of course, advisable to obtain professional advice with a lease.

☐ The shorter the lease, the less security there is for the restaurant and the less its borrowing power.

☐ A longer lease could be used as security against a loan as well as giving you a greater feeling of security.

□ Ask a tax adviser about setting off a large rent deposit against taxes because the period of non-profit making needs to be taken into account.

□ Make sure the rent is right because this is key to a successful restaurant.

The timing from viewing the property to signing the contract

From viewing the property to signing the contract can take from eight to twelve weeks, depending on the complexities of the property and the availability of your finances. The timing can also be affected by your council's efficiency.

If the restaurant is a shell and needs planning permission and licensing, this may take three to five months. Change of use can take one month.

FRANCHISING A BUSINESS

Franchising a restaurant business is still mainly confined to the fast-food market, such as Domino's Pizza, Dunking Donuts and Baskin Robbins. Mid-market franchising has been considered by a few better-quality companies, but little has appeared to date. Franchising, however, can apply to any type of restaurant.

The concept behind franchising is taking a proven format and replicating it. The franchisee invests in setting up the premises (McDonald's set-ups can cost up to £250,000 to kit out one of their outlets) and then shares in the profits.

This is a very safe way of opening a restaurant if being an entrepreneur doesn't appeal to you. Customers come from day one as they know and like the product. Kentucky Fried Chicken is a case in point, as opposed to 'Bert's Fried Chicken'. Ninety-five per cent of franchises are profitable in five years.

Franchising is not for the work-shy. It is extremely hard work, the franchisee is regularly checked and the rules of operation are very strict.

LOCAL GOVERNMENT AND YOUR BUSINESS

Before embarking on any building work, consult your local authority about planning permission, building regulations and any structural changes you wish to make to the property. It is vital to obtain their advice and/or permission before starting on any building.

□ Obtain approval for change of use permission if you are converting a property.

□ Consider consulting a professional to sort out the paperwork if the process is complicated – and for your own peace of mind.

☐ If you feel your application was handled badly, contact the authority first, then a higher authority if you are still dissatisfied. You may wish to discuss the steps you could take with your solicitor or a professional planning consultant.

SCRUTINISING A PROPERTY

Scrutinise properties thoroughly. To help you negotiate a price, the following is a checklist of items you could discuss with the agents:

☐ Are there cracks or any visible structural problems?

☐ Are the ceilings flaking? Damp patches?

☐ Is the flooring, particularly in the kitchen areas, suitable and in good condition?

☐ Is there good drainage?

☐ Does the flooring slope or have holes in it? Is it uneven? Are there changes in floor level?

☐ Are kitchen and equipment surfaces in sound condition?

☐ Is there adequate lighting or will new lighting have to be installed?

☐ Do the stairs have hand rails?

☐ Are the windows in good order? Check for rotting wood.

☐ Is the roof sound?

☐ Does the whole property need to be redecorated?

☐ Is there good ventilation?

☐ Is there an adequate supply of hot water and drinking water?

☐ Is appropriate fire safety equipment installed?

☐ If equipment such as fridges and cookers is included in the deal, is this moveable to clean behind, in good working order, well maintained and clean?

KITCHEN LAYOUT

The design of your kitchen and service areas is of great importance if you are to provide a safe working environment and avoid the cross-contamination of food. Your layout should be built around the operation, not the other way around. Points to consider include the following:

☐ The same basic rules apply irrespective of the size of the establishment.

☐ An old building, such as a seventeenth-century cottage converted into a restaurant, may not have a perfect layout. Decide if the areas can be made to work – or not.

☐ To avoid cross-contamination, there should be a logical flow of delivery, storage, prepping, cooking, serving, disposal of waste and rubbish storage, with as many clearly designated areas for each stage of work as necessary.

For example, someone delivers a box and puts this down on the counter where chicken is being prepared. Not only can the box have dirt on its bottom but it may also now have picked up raw chicken bits. The box may now be moved to another part of the kitchen so that and the cross-contamination enters the second stage. The kitchen counter may also be contaminated from dirt on the box, the box perhaps having been put down on the pavement prior to being taken into the restaurant. All of this can be avoided if a logical flow – and common sense – is adhered to.

☐ Is space limited so that efficiency is impaired?

☐ Is cleaning difficult?

☐ Is there sufficient space to work at benches (i.e. counters) and other fixed equipment to allow people to pass?

☐ To avoid congestion, the layout of cookers, ovens, fryers, refrigeration and machinery with or without moving parts must be taken into account.

Ventilation requirements

Good ventilation creates a comfortable working environment, reduces humidity, and removes contaminated greasy air, steam and cooking smells. It also prevents condensation and will ultimately save on redecoration and maintenance costs.

Cost-cutting on ventilation can result in high temperatures and humidity with an increased risk of food poisoning. Good maintenance is essential if the ventilation is to remain effective. External ducts usually require planning permission and need to be positioned carefully to avoid complaints from your neighbours.

There are three main types of ventilation:

1. **Natural ventilation**: this is only suitable for small-scale operations. This system is seldom ideal because it relies on open windows and doors, is subject to the whims of the weather and is least effective when it is hot. Mesh screening is necessary to keep out flying insects.

2. **Extract-only system**: this is a simple, inexpensive technique which uses an extractor fan to draw out hot or stale air, cooking fumes and steam. It ensures that cooking smells do not spread to other rooms.

3. **Combined extract/inlet system**: this is the most efficient system with the fullest control. It balances the flow of air in and out of the kitchen. It is based on a combination of ducting and fans that remove the hot, damp and sometimes greasy air, replacing this with fresh air.

Hygiene facilities

An adequate water supply, wash basins, sinks, washing-up equipment and good draining are of paramount importance.

Water supply and drainage

Drinkable (also known as potable) water must be used to ensure food is not contaminated. In addition:

☐ Only drinkable water should be used to make ice cubes.

☐ Water from a storage tank or private water supply must be monitored on a regular basis.

☐ In new premises, the drinking-water installation should be disinfected. Your local authority or architect can advise on this.

☐ Drainage facilities must be constructed to avoid the risk of contamination.

☐ All sink, wash basin and dishwasher pipes should discharge directly into the drainage system through a trapped gully to prevent foul odours. Because this involves floor channels, deep seal gullies and sewers, contact your local authority for further information.

Sinks and washing-up equipment

Facilities for food preparation, staff use, crockery, general cleaning and the disinfecting of work tools and equipment all require a supply of hot and cold water and must be easily cleanable and well sited.

☐ Lavatories must not be next to a food-handling space.

☐ Hand-washing facilities must be provided in prep areas, with hot and cold water and materials for cleaning hands.

☐ Sinks for washing food must be separate from hand-washing sinks.

☐ Separate hand wash basins are preferable in each work and food service area, including the bar, and also at the entrance to the kitchen.

☐ Stainless-steel wash basins are strongly recommended but glazed ceramic basins are acceptable. Domestic sinks are not acceptable.

☐ Wash basins with foot, knee, 'automatic operated' or mixer taps are a good idea but are not necessary.

☐ Hand dryers should be positioned carefully so that dirt and bacteria aren't blown around food areas. Because they are slow and inefficient, thus perhaps putting off frequent hand washing, disposable towels are the best bet.

☐ One or more commercial-quality stainless-steel sinks are recommended for the main sinks, with one or more deep sinks for pot washing.

☐ In large catering premises separate sinks are required for each of the following: vegetables, salads, meat and fish.

☐ A dishwashing machine with a fitted water softener (for certain hard-water areas) is recommended for all but the smallest of food premises. Commercial dishwashers take very little time in comparison with domestic dishwashers and are designed with a simple interior and controls.

☐ A sink with a double stainless-steel (never wooden) drainer is also recommended and may be used instead of a dishwasher, but why be hard on yourself?

☐ The bar might have a glass-washing machine and/or a sink (single/double) with a double drainer.

☐ A separate sink for mops, buckets, etc., should be located outside the food area.

These are recommendations only. Take advice from your environmental health officer, particularly if you have small premises with little space.

Refuse storage

Even restaurants like Rick Stein's seafood restaurant in Padstow have difficulties with rubbish due to lack of space outside. If you have the space, position free-standing bins well away from the diners' view because this can be very off-putting. Some restaurants don't follow this aesthetically pleasing advice so, if you want repeat business, hide the bins strategically if possible.

☐ Don't allow food waste and other refuse to accumulate in food rooms.

☐ Waste must be put into closed, sound, easy-to-clean containers.

☐ Free-standing or wall-mounted lidded holders for plastic bags should be provided, or a foot-operated plastic-lidded bin lined with a plastic bag.

☐ Remove full bags and clean the containers and surrounding area frequently.

☐ Refuse storage and removal must be protected from pests (flying insects, cats, dogs and foxes in particular) and must not contaminate the premises, drinking water or equipment.

☐ Either site your refuse storage externally with a roofed cover if space allows, or in a non-food area with plenty of ventilation.

☐ Keep wheeliebins clean and mark these clearly with your restaurant's name.

☐ Bulk collection of refuse can be arranged for the larger business. One large London restaurant uses 120 local-authority-paid bags a week at a cost of over £1,500 a year. Pigswill bins, bottles and boxes are collected by another firm. The pigswill is 'cooked' in vats by steam and fed to pigs. Contact your local authority to find out what type of service they offer and the costs. Also, contact them for the disposal of white goods (fridges and freezers, for example).

Pest control

Avoiding infestations of rodents, insects and other food pests is a priority:

☐ Any infestation will lead to the contamination of food and food surfaces, and to damage to food stocks and the building.

☐ Maintain high standards of cleanliness, housekeeping, food storage and vermin proofing of the building.

☐ Problems with cockroaches, mice, pharaoh ants (tiny brown ants) and rats can all be dealt with by local authority or private contractor exterminators.

☐ The cleaner your restaurant – and this includes behind fridges, etc., where vermin love to congregate – the fewer problems you'll encounter.

 Gloss paint encourages condensation, artex ceilings are not acceptable due to difficulty with cleaning and polystyrene or acoustic tiles are unlikely to be passed by inspectors. Ceiling tiles should be fire retardant.

FIRST IMPRESSIONS

First impressions are vital:

☐ Is your restaurant welcoming and well kept?

☐ Is it well lit?

☐ Is there any cracked paint?

☐ Are the windows clean, the entrance swept and the door handles polished?

☐ Are the menu and times of opening visible?

☐ Is the entrance to the car park clearly signed?

☐ If you have a garden and paths, are they well maintained?

If you ignore these, the customers will go elsewhere. If your property looks dirty, they'll wonder what the kitchens and toilets are like.

 Keep your entrance clutter-free for the easy access of able-bodied and disabled customers alike.

LICENCES

Alcohol licences

The Licensing Act 2003 permits flexible opening hours for licensed premises, with the opportunity for 24-hour opening, seven days a week, subject to a consideration of the impact on local residents. The aim is to minimise public disorder resulting from fixed closing times. The Act also provides a single scheme for licensing premises that sell alchohol, provide public entertainment or provide refreshment late at night.

Pubs, restaurants, businesses serving hot food between 11 am and 5 pm, hotels, guest houses and other businesses that sell alcohol all require a **premises licence**.

A **personal licence** is needed by anyone who allows the sale of alcohol. This is valid for ten years. There are various duties on the holders of personal licences, and the court can cancel your licence if you are convicted of certain offences. To obtain a personal licence you must be over 18, not have any relevant criminal convictions as spelt out in the Act, possess an approved licensing qualification and pay the required fee.

The four licensing objectives are:

1. the prevention of crime and disorder;

2. the prevention of public nuisance;

3. public safety; and

4. the prevention of harm to children.

Premises licences

A premise licence can be granted either for a one-off event or indefinitely. Applicants have to submit a plan of their building, an operating schedule (a brief description of how the premises will be operated safely) and a fee (in the region of £500 maximum). Contact your local authority to find out the cost.

Temporary and occasional events

Licences will not be needed for small events where fewer than 500 people are likely to attend and the event lasts for less than 72 hours. Someone with a personal licence is able to hold up to 50 temporary or occasional events a year at other premises that are not licensed. Non-personal licence holders are able to hold up to five temporary events a year. A **temporary event notice** must be given to the council before such an event can be held, and the police may object to it on crime and disorder grounds.

Contact your district council for guidance on how to obtain a licence and your local trading standards officer for alcohol measurement guidelines.

Public entertainment licences

If music, entertainment or dancing are to be held, a public entertainment licence may be required. Contact your environmental health officer, who will also give you advice on the prevention of noise nuisance.

Notification of accidents

Under the Reporting of Injuries, Diseases and Occurences Regulations 1995, employers must contact the environmental health office about any fatality, major injury, accident or dangerous occurrence that happens on their premises.

Fire certification

Some types of food businesses require a fire certificate. Consult your local fire-prevention officer.

MUSIC

Music can enhance the atmosphere of a restaurant, putting people in the mood for a good time as soon as they enter the door. Conversely, it can alienate your customers. If they need to shout to be heard, this is clearly unacceptable. If your restaurant's atmosphere has hushed tones you may wish to inject some suitable music, but remember to listen to your customers. Often silence, that rare commodity, is golden.

If you play recorded music you will need to have a licence from the Performing Rights Society. The fee applies to performances in the UK of copyright music within the society's remit at hotels, restaurants, cafés, fast-food outlets, banqueting suites, function rooms, boarding houses and guesthouses. Currently, only theatre restaurants, theatre cafés and similar premises are exempt.

For advice, email musiclicence@prs.co.uk, contact www.prs.co.uk or call (0800) 068 48 28. For live music, see 'Licences' above.

SMOKING

From 1 July 2007, smoking in any enclosed public space, such as a restaurant, pub, hospital or office was prohibited. Businesses face fines of up £20,500 if they break the law. This applies to all parts of the UK.

The ban includes smoking anything containing tobacco, including pipes, cigars and hand-rolled cigarettes. The law states the following:

   □ The new smoke-free law applies to virtually all 'enclosed' and 'substantially enclosed' public spaces and workplaces. This includes both permanent structures and temporary ones, such as tents and marquees. Thus also means that indoor smoking rooms in public places and workplaces is no longer allowed.

□ Premises will be considered 'enclosed' if they have a ceiling or roof and (except for doors, windows or passageways) are wholly enclosed either on a permanent or temporary basis.

□ Premises will be considered 'substantially enclosed' if they have a ceiling or roof but have an opening in the walls which is less than half the total area of the walls. The area of the opening does not include doors, windows or any other fittings that can be opened or shut.

□ There is no requirement for outdoor smoking shelters to be provided for employees or members of the public.

If you do decide to build a shelter, discuss any plans you may have with your local council as there may be a range of issues you need to consider. These might include planning permission, licensing, building control, noise and litter.

For more information about smoking legislation, go to the Office of Public Sector Information's website (www.opsi.gov.uk).

Work with your solicitor or bookkeeper to create a system for alerting you when your licences need to be renewed. Make licences a priority for the good health of your business – and your customers.

COMPLYING WITH ACTS
Disabled access and facilities
Consult your planning department regarding disabled access, space within your restaurant and toilets designed for wheelchair access. An existing restaurant in an eighteenth-century building, for example, may not need to have a ramp, but new builds have to conform with the disability laws.

Amendments to the Disability Discrimination Act 1995, which came into force in October 2004, require you to address any physical features which make it difficult to use your restaurant. These include:

□ steps, stairways and kerbs;

□ parking, exterior surfaces and paving;

□ building entrances and signage;

□ toilet and washing facilities;

□ public facilities; and

□ lifts and escalators.

In some cases it may be unreasonable as a result of cost or planning legislation to make these changes. Contact your local authority or the Papworth Trust (www.papworth.org.uk) to find out about the requirements, guide dogs for the blind and other issues that affect disabled people. For further information, go to www.disability.gov.uk.

There are eight and a half million disabled people in the UK, with one in four customers being disabled or being close to someone who is.

☐ Plan ahead to meet the requirements of your disabled customers.

☐ Don't make assumptions about disabled people based on speculation and stereotypes.

☐ Have a positive policy of providing services to disabled customers and staff.

Sale of Goods and Trades Description Acts

As a trader you must be aware of the Sale of Goods Act, which states that there is an unexpressed contract when you accept a customer's order. The customer may either demand a replacement or refuse to pay. For example:

☐ If the goods don't correspond with the description (e.g., roast chicken which has been poached instead of being roasted).

☐ If artificial cream is offered instead of fresh cream.

☐ If the food is inedible.

It makes no difference if the customer has partly or wholly consumed the food – the Trades Description Act makes it a criminal offence to describe goods or services incorrectly. Watch out for the following:

☐ The wording on menus and wine lists.

☐ Describing food and drink to customers verbally.

☐ Describing services, eg. cover and service charges or extras.

☐ Describing services on offer.

If someone is charged under the Act, the defence is to prove that reasonable precautions were taken and that the alleged offence:

☐ was the result of a pure mistake;

☐ was the result of information from someone else;

□ was the fault of someone else;

□ was the result of an accident or other cause beyond the control of the person concerned; or

□ was committed by a person who could not reasonably know the description was misleading.

For the trading standards alcohol requirements, see Chapter 11.

Discrimination

The Sex Discrimination Act and the Race Relations Act both legislate against discrimination on the grounds of colour, race, creed or sex.

□ Refusing service to customers of a particular colour, race, creed or sex.

□ Refusing services by imposing unjustifiable conditions or requirements on these same groups of people.

□ Victimisation by refusing entry, providing a poorer service than that offered to the general public or that may only be available at a price premium.

The Hotel Proprietors Act

A hotel's management is under no obligation to serve anyone apart from customers staying at the hotel or similar establishment. The reasons for refusal include the following:

□ There is no space left.

□ The person is drunk.

□ The person is under the influence of drugs.

□ The person is not suitably dressed.

□ The person is a known trouble-maker.

□ The person is an associate of a known trouble-maker.

□ The person is under the legal minimum age for licensed premises or does not fit into the age policy set by the premises.

□ Under the Licensed Premises (Exclusion of Certain Persons) Act 1980 the licensee has the right to refuse entry to people who are drunk, violent and disorderly, quarrelsome or who appear unable to pay.

□ It is an offence to sell intoxicating liquor to a drunk person or those under 18 years of age.

PRICE MARKING (FOOD AND DRINK ON PREMISES) ORDER 2003

This order came into in 2004 and outlines the following:

☐ 'Eating area' means any part of any premises specifically set aside and equipped for the consumption of food notwithstanding that some other activity may be carried on in the area in question but does not include a supply area.

☐ 'Food' means food and drink for human consumption but does not include food which is supplied

— (a) at the express request of a purchaser in a case where the seller has not indicated that food of the same description is or may be for sale by him; or

— (b) at a price agreed in advance pursuant to an order made before an intending purchaser enters the eating area, supply area or take-away area in question to obtain or consume the food.

☐ 'Premises' includes any vehicle or vessel.

☐ 'Soft drink' means any non-alcoholic drink of a kind which is served cold.

☐ 'Supply area' means any part of any premises specifically set aside and equipped for the supply of food in a case where an intending purchaser pays for food for consumption on the premises where it is sold before it is consumed notwithstanding that some activity may be carried on in the area in question.

☐ 'Take-away area' means any part of any premises specifically set aside and equipped for the supply of food heated at the request of a consumer or supplied as heated meals in each case for consumption off the premises where it is sold notwithstanding in any case that some other activity may be carried on in the area in question.

☐ 'Wine' means any drink obtained from the alcoholic fermentation of fresh grapes or the must of fresh grapes other than drink fortified with spirits or flavoured with aromatic extracts.

The prices of food and drink must be displayed in a clear and legible way by persons selling food by retail for consumption on the premises, but this does not apply to members of a club or their guests, in staff restaurants or in guesthouses. Private catering menus are also excluded.

A menu and drinks list must be placed at the entrance or be able to be read from the street. If the restaurant is part of a hotel complex, the list must be shown at the entrance to the eating area. Both food and drink must be included. Table d'hôte (set menu) prices must be given. VAT must be included, and a service and/or a cover charge must be shown as an amount or a percentage.

In self-service premises where the customer chooses food, the prices must be shown at the entrance unless they can be seen at the counter.

YOUR CHECKLIST

Ask yourself the following:

☐ Have you registered your premises?

☐ Do the design and construction of your premises meet legal requirements?

☐ Have you considered all the health and fire-safety requirements?

☐ Do you and your staff understand the principles of good food hygiene?

☐ Have you and your staff had food-hygiene training?

☐ Have you considered what food-safety problems there could be at each stage of the business?

☐ Have you put the necessary food-safety procedures in place and are you making regular checks to ensure they are working?

☐ Do you describe food and drink accurately?

☐ Do you need to apply for a licence to sell alcohol?

☐ Have you registered as self-employed?

☐ Do you need to register for VAT?

☐ Are you keeping records of all your business income and expenses?

☐ Are you keeping records of your employees' pay and deductions for their tax and National Insurance contributions?

4

FINANCING YOUR BUSINESS

As Kit Chapman, restaurateur/owner of the Castle Hotel, Taunton, and the Brazz brasseries says, 'making money is the first priority.'

Other reasons for opening a restaurant include creating a business that suits your personality, offering hospitality and being in a vibrant trade. Is opening a restaurant a romantic ideal or a profitable business proposal? Can the two meet?

CREATING INCOME

The advice of successful restaurateurs is never to lose sight of your livelihood – and that of your partners, family and staff. Wise words. It is so seductive being your own boss in this entertainment/food world that it is quite easy to lose sight of your prime consideration: your income.

Curb your naturally generous instincts with friends when they visit your restaurant. It is all very well offering wine on the house, a meal, coffees. They may come to expect it. Instead, become shrewd, be aware of margins and rein in your bountiful nature.

Take a leaf out of corporate industries' practice and have a loss leader on the menu. Shop around for good-quality produce and equipment rather than succumbing at the first shopping expedition. Negotiate. Haggle. This still does happen in the western world. Be armed with good information, prices and an understanding of the market when dealing with any part of your restaurant's finances.

In the honeymoon period the curiosity value of a new restaurant brings in diners. Once this is over the finance part of the business may need to be revised and long-term strategies with stages of development built into the picture.

Steps to developing a financial base

Some restaurants don't lose that honeymoon period but create enough interest to attract a growing band of loyal and new customers. They continue to develop a working financial base and put into practice the art of producing consistent quality food, good service, conviviality, atmosphere and value for money. Constantly analysing, updating and reinventing your business is as important as never losing sight of the art of hospitality.

This finance chapter deals with:

☐ raising capital;

☐ creating a business plan;

☐ forming a company;

☐ planning overheads;

☐ trading projections;

☐ financial records; and

☐ tips.

National minimum wage payments, pensions and other staff issues are in Chapter 8.

A BUSINESS PLAN

First, you need to work out your initial proposal for the type of restaurant you wish to run. For example:

☐ Its name, location and concept.

☐ Who your customers will be.

☐ What is on your menu and drinks list.

☐ Your staffing and purchase costings, rental and projected income per day.

Business plans are recommended by most experts, and banks in particular demand them for further discussion. However, many entrepreneurs operate without them. If you are not completely sure that your restaurant will work without one, however, then think of a business plan as being an asset, one of your strengths.

These plans are, of course, not a guarantee for success but, by identifying your strengths and weaknesses, you will greatly improve your chances of succeeding. The plan, however, needs updating as it is a working tool. It's your map to success.

To build on the initial proposal, follow these steps:

☐ **Executive summary**: describe the business in general terms on approximately one page.

☐ **Overview**: your mission. What are you looking to achieve? Why do you think it will work?

☐ **Introduction**: your restaurant's purpose, your expertise and history, and those of your partners and your staff (should you have a chef lined up, for example), and your critical success factors (what is going to make it work).

☐ **Business environment**: your market research into your type of restaurant, its location potential, problems and possible solutions, the competition and an expansion potential (running outside catering, for example).

☐ **Make your presentation professional-looking**: a messy jumble of ideas randomly put on paper will not improve anyone's chances of getting to the next stage of discussions. Instead, choose a business-like font, put ideas under headings, check the spelling and present it in a titled folder with perhaps some clear drawings. Make several copies to hand out.

FORMING A COMPANY

If you decide to operate as a company, you will have to pay corporation tax and submit company tax returns. The corporation tax self-assessment form available from the Inland Revenue deals with this. Soon after the end of the accounting period they will send you a notice asking you to submit a company tax return.

You must normally pay any tax due by nine months and one day after the end of the accounting period. If you have not yet completed your company tax return you must make an estimate of what you think is due and pay that.

Send your completed tax return, including your accounts and tax computations, to the Inland Revenue by the filing date, which is usually 12 months after the end of the accounting period. If the return is not delivered by this date, you will incur a penalty.

Maintain proper business records and keep these for six years after the end of the accounting period. Speak to your accountant or tax adviser to decide on the accounting period and tell your tax office. Work out the dates by which you need to pay tax and submit your company tax return.

Plan ahead to make sure that accounts and tax computations are prepared in good time, but always communicate with your tax office if you fall behind. Make sure it's a two-way dialogue for your peace of mind.

CALCULATING MENU COSTINGS AND PRICES

Getting menu pricing wrong has been the downfall of many a new restaurant and, as a general rule of thumb, successful restaurants work on a 65 per cent gross profit (GP), excluding VAT. Once you have calculated the costs of any dish, multiply these by 3.3. You can't go too far wrong but, of course, there are exceptions to the 65 per cent GP rule.

To calculate your GP margin, first work out the cost of each dish on the menu. Obtain price lists from wholesale companies and other suppliers, including pricing goods at retail shops, farm shops, specialist mail-order food companies and other sources (such as van drivers delivering produce in your area).

If you are going to specialise in fresh fish, for example, are there any good suppliers in your area or do you need to source quality fish from further away? Ask a friendly, trustworthy restaurateur whom they use and look up fish suppliers in *Yellow Pages* in your area and further afield (e.g. London and Brixham).

 The set-up costs can be frightening. Don't be put off. You have to spend money to make money.

Working out the costs

Calculate everything that goes into that particular recipe, including the garnishes, the butter the fish might be cooked in, the VAT and the time involved to make the dish. It obviously takes longer to make a real lemon tart than to scoop out bought-in ice cream.

Ask yourself the following after calculating the recipe costs and menu prices:

☐ Can the market withstand my pricing?

☐ What is the competition like?

 If you are buying an existing business, approach the business figures with caution. They may not always be as buoyant as they appear. Study them carefully and ask pertinent questions.

At the beginning of your business, there could be a degree of wastage which will have an impact on your GP margins, but this will be resolved with good management practices once your business gets going.

Some items will be cheaper than others to prepare. Offset more expensive dishes by lowering the GP on these dishes and increasing the GP on the cheaper dishes. For example, it is difficult to make 65 per cent GP on some dishes that use expensive meat, game, shellfish, fish and foie gras. This is loss-leader practice and will help to increase the sales of the more expensive item, but shore up the cost by making a larger GP on cheaper dishes.

Before the net profit is calculated the cost of overheads is deducted from the GP, including wages and running costs, leaving you with an average profit of 10 to 15 per cent. Then deduct the loan repayments, interest and tax.

Bear in mind that interest rates can vary and that the amounts paid to staff, the owner and partners are equally unknown in the initial stages of the business.

Wine bar/restaurant trading projections

Mon-Thurs	Covers	Cost	Multiply by	Total
Morning coffee	20	£3	4	£240
T/o lunch*	20	£4.50	4	£360
Lunch	15	£10	4	£600
Evening meal	20	£25	4	£2,000
Wine bar	20	£5.50	4	£440
Total				£3,640

Friday	Covers	Cost	Multiply by	Total
Morning coffee	30	£3	1	£90
T/o lunch	20	£4.50	1	£90
Lunch	20	£10	1	£200
Evening meal	40	£25	1	£1,000
Wine bar	50	£7.50	1	£375
Total				£1,755

Saturday	Covers	Cost	Multiply by	Total
Morning coffee	35	£4	1	£140
T/o lunch	10	£4.50	1	£45
Lunch	45	£10	1	£450
Evening meal	45	£25	1	£1,125
Wine bar	50	£10	1	£500
Total				£2,260

Sunday	Covers	Cost	Multiply by	Total
Breakfast/brunch	20	£8.50	1	£170
Lunch	40	£15	1	£600
Wine bar	30	£10	1	£300
Total				£1,070

Total for the week	£8,725
Monthly average	£37,808

*T/O: take-out lunch

Monthly costs

Rent/rates	£2,500	Laundry	£300
Wages	£8,000	Breakages	£200
Food	£10,000	Promotion	£500
Wine	£600		
Utilities	£750		
Loan servicing	£2,500		
		Total	£25,350

Monthly average less monthly costs £12,458 less VAT @ 17.5% = £10,602

Cover charges, menu supplement charges and service charges

These charges can sound alarm bells in customers' minds: when they see extra charges for bread, steep pricing for vegetables and the so-called optional service charge on the menu and when they ask for the bill and see hidden charges added on to the total.

You may lose customers while they are scrutinising your menu: they will think twice about going through your door. The resentment that is caused by hidden charges will rocket when those charges are there in black and white on the bill. Customers who feel they have been ripped off will not return. Customers naturally prefer to know in advance about all the charges.

Cover charge

The old-fashioned cover charge is sadly alive and well. It is mainly found in tourist hot spots where unsuspecting tourists may not notice it. The restaurant covers itself by saying it is for linen, glasses and staff. Really, any excuse will do. But then that same restaurant will charge for bread and add a service charge. This is an iniquitous charge that countless customers – and, to be fair, many restaurateurs – find totally unacceptable.

Raise your prices very slowly.

Extra charges

A medium-range Portsmouth fish restaurant I once reviewed had a nice little greedy policy: charge them for the sauces to go with the fish, charge them for the bread and the vegetables on already high prices and slap on a 15 per cent service charge. The price per head for a very dull, two-course meal at this restaurant was the same as a superb, three-course set menu at Gordon Ramsay's Royal Hospital Road, London, restaurant at lunchtime.

If you feel you must charge for bread, then make sure it is excellent bread. If you feel you must charge for any extras, offer the very best produce if you want repeat business.

Service charge

The service charge is a tricky area and there are no legal guidelines on how you charge for service. This charge (added to the bill before VAT is added), is usually 12½ per cent of the bill, although it does rise to 15 per cent. The word 'discretionary' usually comes before this percentage. However, most people pay up without fuss and don't query the charge.

This is very common practice and, in lower-priced restaurants, may be a fixed amount added to the bill, but in many restaurants it is 12½ per cent. Some restaurants pass it on to their staff (waiting and kitchen) if wages are low or it is considered part of the restaurant's revenue if the staff are better paid.

Most staff, however, prefer tips and a distribution of the charge. But customers are waking up to the fact that, if they pay the service charge, they don't need to leave a tip. Why pay twice? They assume that the service charge is just that: money going directly to the waiting staff.

Customers are within their rights not to pay the service charge if they have been let down by poor service. This, of course, may not be the fault of the waiting staff but the slowness of the kitchen. My advice is to remove the service charge without quibbling if the customer asks for this.

Voluntary service charges

There is great concern within the hospitality industry that many diners are feeling they have been tricked into paying twice for service by restaurants who leave credit-card slips blank for tips. Trading standards officers report that many customers are being caught out because of the widespread use of credit cards. A survey done in London by trading standards inspectors found that half of the 68 restaurants visited left the credit-card slip open for a gratuity, despite already adding a service charge.

Restaurants that impose voluntary service charges are in breach of a code of practice brought in alongside the Consumer Protection Act 1987, which seeks to abolish the charges and have them incorporated into a single bill.

If restaurants fail to show the cost of eating out clearly and legibly, this can result in fines of £5,000. Trading Standards are not looking to ban service charges but want to ensure that customers have a real choice of whether to pay – or not.

Conclusion

An optional service charge is acceptable, but the practice of leaving a credit-card slip blank for a tip when the customer has already paid for service is not.

A duped customer will view this as one of the most objectionable aspects about dining out, and it can sour a very good restaurant experience. Avoid following this sadly widespread, underhand practice.

When you start in business, keep your prices below the competition but your quality higher.

TIPPING

Some £4 billion is left in tips a year, and with different restaurants having different policies over tips and service charges, it is no wonder customers and employees are confused. Some customers leave 12.5 per cent, others others 10 or even 15 per cent. What is left as cash goes to the staff. A tip on plastic goes to the restaurant, which may or may not decide to pass it on to the staff. Under the 'tronc' system, cash tips are pooled and distributed equally by a designated member of staff.

A campaign organised by the union Unite wants restaurants to pay all their workers at least the minimum working wage plus 100 per cent of all tips. Some restaurants use tips to top up to the minimum wage. The Institute of Hospitality has set out new minimum wage and tipping regulations, and the European Court of Human Rights is on the case.

ATTRACTING FINANCE

To attract financing it pays to have the following:

☐ sales goals;

☐ customer profiles;

☐ the right economic environment (is there an economic slump or boom?);

☐ knowledge of trends in the restaurant trade;

☐ an analysis of the competition;

☐ a marketing strategy;

☐ key person resumés – you and your partner's strengths and background;

□ your chef's background and expertise (if you have a chef);

□ a cash-flow projection;

□ revenue projections;

□ taxation projections – VAT included;

□ your financing requirements: amount needed, a detailed budget, your repayment options; and

□ bank documents.

Again, this vital paperwork needs to be well presented in titled folders and handed out with confidence.

RAISING CAPITAL AND OBTAINING BUSINESS PARTNERS/INVESTORS

Aim to raise more money than you need. You often have only one chance of raising money, so take a close look at what you think you will need. It is very difficult to ask the same source the second time around for more funding. If your figures are too conservative, this may ultimately mean that your business proposition is not viable.

Raising the money

Your bank is not your only port of call. There may be better and cheaper ways of raising finance. Work out exactly how much you need and for how long. Re-mortgaging your house may not be suitable if you need money for the short term. If you need money to buy equipment, look at renting and leasing options.

If you do choose to go down the bank route, shop around. The competition between banks is intense, so look around at the deals on offer. Negotiate: don't accept proposals for what they are. Stipulate your needs and offer a rate of interest to the time you can start paying back the loan. However, banks can be wary of lending money to new restaurant ventures because their track record is less than successful.

There is no rule that says you have to bank with the bank that gives you a loan. Perhaps there are better deals at another bank. And if the loan comes from a bank that doesn't have a high-street presence or is too far away from your business to make it practical to pay money in, then this may be yet another reason for banking elsewhere. The bank that has lent you the money will respect your good business sense.

WORKING IN A PARTNERSHIP

Are you going into business alone or with a partner? Or will you be forming a company with investors or lenders? The latter is the route taken by most small restaurants. Try to achieve majority control, with your partners or investors as minor shareholders. You will, however, have to convince them that you are capable of running such a business.

Keep the people who matter in the know. Your partners must be completely up to date with any transactions you may have made on behalf of the business. Communication is all when dealing with partners and those who fund your restaurant if you wish to stay in business.

Choose your partners or investors with care. Discuss your plans in great detail. Are they on the same wavelength as you? Do they have the same aspirations and goals? What strengths do they possess? Be aware of the investor who wishes to run the business because they know better. This can only lead to tears and a messy falling-out. Look for investors and/or partners who respect your strengths and weaknesses, and vice versa. Clearly define the areas of responsibility at the onset. These may shift as the business progresses, but discuss these changes in full when they arise.

When entering into a partnership, outline and protect personal investment as well as the agreed split of assets and liabilities. Get it down on paper and obtain a lawyer (see 'Legal Tips' later in this chapter).

CAPITAL EXPENDITURE

Look at the capital costs before searching for funding and work out the figures for each cost. Remember, if your figures are too conservative, it will be difficult to return to the same source for more funding. Guesswork will be involved in these calculations because not all the figures can be established correctly, so a contingency fund is needed.

The lists below for capital expenditure for a restaurant/bar can be adapted to suit your own specific business.

The property
Consider the following expenditure:

☐ rent deposit, on-going rent or cost to buy;

☐ renovations, including labour and materials;

☐ building costs and labour;

☐ plumbing, electrical labour and materials;

☐ décor, including any artefacts;

☐ a toilet upgrade;

☐ accountant's and bookkeeper's fees;

☐ bar construction and furbishing;

☐ chairs, tables and service area costs;

☐ floor covering and window blinds/curtains;

☐ lighting;

☐ heating, air conditioning and kitchen extractor fan; and

☐ fire extinguishers.

Kitchen and restaurant equipment
You may need:

☐ large and small kitchen equipment, including rental equipment;

☐ glass, cutlery and crockery;

☐ a coffee espresso machine – lease or buy;

☐ cleaning equipment, including vacuum cleaners and window cleaners;

☐ a rubbish-removal service;

☐ linen, napkins, glass cloths, kitchen uniforms and waiting staff uniforms;

☐ a laundry service;

☐ a music system, speakers, recorded music and performing rights licences;

☐ a cash register;

☐ opening stocks: food, alcohol, cleaning materials;

☐ an opening party.

Ancillary costs

These will include:

- ☐ telephones;

- ☐ gas and electricity;

- ☐ office equipment;

- ☐ printing for menus, cards, publicity handouts, bill heads;

- ☐ advertising;

- ☐ promotion;

- ☐ graphics;

- ☐ menu research, including travel; and

- ☐ exterior lighting and menu boards.

Accountancy and other costs, including legal fees

Budget for:

- ☐ accountant's and bookkeeper's fees;

- ☐ legal fees;

- ☐ rates;

- ☐ insurance;

- ☐ permits: fire, health, business licence;

- ☐ licence fees;

- ☐ staff costs – waiting, kitchen, cleaning, office;

- ☐ breakages;

- ☐ operating capital; and

- ☐ a contingency fund.

NEXT STEPS IN FINDING FUNDING

With your capital cost figures under your belt and armed with a business plan and your initial trading proposal, it's time to persuade others to fund your venture. Whether your capital will come from the bank or a private investor, your lender is looking for your business to survive in order to recoup the loan and the agreed interest. The lender needs to be satisfied that the business has the right people at the helm, that its location is sound and that good research into the projected customer base has been undertaken.

Bookkeeping and accountancy

It is essential to put in place good bookkeeping practices right from the beginning so that investors, accountants and the Inland Revenue can see at a glance your cash flow, expenses and profit and loss margins.

Store all your transactions on a computer because this will give you immediate information about your operation: the sales, its mix, stock turnover, sales per table and waiter (very useful for checking facts if needed), food and drink cost percentages. Computers also offer a cost-effective way of reducing paperwork, but bookkeeping (nowadays usually a software package) is still essential, so do add the cost of employing a bookkeeper/accountant on to the capital costs. Choose an accountant who has experience and a liking for the restaurant trade. Do a cash-flow forecast together.

Bookkeeping and accountancy requirements

Record cash and bank transactions, weekly sales of all aspects of the business (food and alcohol sales, for example) and weekly payments (suppliers, wages, rent, etc.). Record the weekly income and expenditure on printouts or summary sheets so that you can see at a glance where the money is going out and coming in.

Your accountant will also require information regarding VAT, tips, credit-card and cash sales, wages, purchases, operating costs (rent, rates, utilities, telephone, laundry, for example), drawings for investors and owners, and capital costs (maintenance, repairs, improvements).

Breaking the business down into the sum of its parts can be of immense help to see where your business is going, its strengths and weaknesses, its seasonal swings. It can also be helpful in combating fraud and theft (see the tips on page 46).

At the end of the financial year (March 31), two summaries should be prepared: the trading profit and loss accounts showing the gross profit, and the net profit and the balance sheet showing the company's financial position. The latter shows the assets owned and the debts owed. The difference between the two is the capital value of the business, which represents the capital invested by the owner/investors and the retained profits.

VALUE ADDED TAX (VAT)

Value Added Tax (VAT) is charged on most business transactions made in the UK and the Isle of Man. VAT is also charged on goods and some services imported from outside the European Union and on goods and some services coming into the UK from the other EU countries.

All goods and services that are VAT rated are called 'taxable supplies'. You must charge VAT on your taxable supplies from the date you first need to be registered. The value of these supplies is called your 'taxable turnover'.

There are currently three rates of VAT:

☐ **17.5 per cent**: the standard rate on most goods and services.

☐ **5 per cent**: the reduced rate on fuel and power used in the home and by charities.

☐ **0 per cent**: applied to non-chargeable items (for example, most food, books, newspapers and children's clothing).

Registering for VAT

You must register for VAT if you are in business and your taxable turnover, not just your profit, goes over a certain limit. The current VAT registration threshold is £67,000 (January 2010) but you can opt to register for VAT if your taxable turnover (the amount going through the business, not just the profit) is less than this if what you do counts as a business for VAT purposes. Taxable turnover is £660,000.

The benefits of registering under the limit include increased credibility for your business but, once you are registered, you will have to account for output tax on all your taxable supplies that are not zero rated. You can, however, take credit for any input tax on those taxable supplies.

You will also have to send in VAT returns regularly and keep proper records and accounts so that the VAT officers can examine them if necessary.

VAT accounting

For small businesses, there are a number of simplified arrangements to make VAT accounting easier:

☐ **Cash accounting**: if your taxable turnover is under £660,000 a year, you can arrange to account to Customs for VAT on the basis of cash received and paid rather than the invoice date or time of supply.

□ **Annual accounting**: if your turnover is under £660,00 a year, you can join the annual accounting scheme and send in just one return a year, rather than the quarterly returns which most businesses do.

□ **Bad-debt relief**: if you supply goods or services to a customer but you are not paid, you may be able to claim relief from VAT on the debts.

□ **Flat-rate scheme**: you may be eligible for the flat-rate scheme if your turnover is under £150,000. This helps save on administration by not accounting internally for VAT on each individual 'in and out'. Payment is over a set percentage of the total turnover.

Ten top tips for simplifying VAT for small businesses

1. Registering for VAT may have major implications on your pricing structure, so always incorporate these into any costings.

2. Apply to register in plenty of time so that you obtain the help available to you, and also obtain your VAT number in good time for printing it on to cards, invoices, etc.

3. Calculate the impact of VAT on your growing business turnover.

4. Good bookkeeping is vital for overall business management. Check the documents you receive. You must have a VAT invoice to claim back VAT. A statement is not a proper invoice.

5. Always enter cash receipts in your books before using the cash to make purchases.

6. Many businesses take advantage of the VAT they've collected, making it work for them before being paid to Customs. Pay the VAT into a separate bank account to accumulate interest. Be sure to keep the VAT collections for payment only to Customs and not for other purposes.

7. If you find yourself unable to send your VAT return or payment on time, call Customs on 0845 010 9000 and tell them why.

8. Consider making a part payment to reduce the surcharge payment.

9. Always quote your VAT number on correspondence, otherwise delays/confusion will occur.

10. If you are not sure, ask. This is in both your and Customs' interests. If in doubt, shout!

PAYROLL

Records must be kept of all staff, whether full or part time. Avoid the temptation to pay unrecorded cash for labour because the penalties for income fraud are severe. The following are necessary for you to keep records:

☐ The employee's name and address.

☐ Their tax code number and National Insurance number.

☐ Tips earned. Restaurateurs are responsible for all income earned, tips included. Tax inspectors can estimate tip earnings if no service charge is included.

INSURANCE

Insurance is a very simple concept. Your annual payment will provide insurance for your business to cover the building, contents and liability, the latter for any litigation (a dispute or lawsuit brought against your business, for example). Even if you are able to cover the costs of replacement or repair or any loss that may occur, such as a shelf giving way with a hundred plates tumbling to the floor, it would be irresponsible not to be insured against customers' legal actions.

Your biggest risk may be from your customers breaking or stealing items, but this may also apply to your staff. There is similarly the possibility of customers or staff falling in your restaurant, and the building itself should be assessed for safety.

Insurance details to look out for

The duty of disclosure is vitally important when confirming and agreeing to the conditions of a policy. The insurer must know what you wish to cover because the type of policy required should be an accurate reflection of your business. Be clear and specific and ask for written confirmation in all areas of your cover. Ask your local authority about insurance requirements.

Spend time talking to the right insurers – those dealing in restaurant/hotel businesses – and obtain several quotes. Ask those who are in the restaurant business whom they recommend or contact an insurance broker. Factor insurance into your overall costings.

Public liability

Public liability covers injury and property damage caused by your personal negligence and/or business negligence.

Product liability

Product liability relates to any products you provide but specifically to the food you serve, either bought in or cooked on the premises. Should a customer find a nail in a roll (yes, it happened to me), you are liable.

Manager liability

Manager liability covers you for your staff looking after your customers in your absence. Customers could not only sue you and your business but also the staff representing you at the time.

Obtaining the right cover

Your policy should include fire, storm, tempest (however ancient this terminology is), burglary, malicious damage and glass breakage.

Additional cover you may wish to consider is business interruption, which replaces lost income in the event of a disaster that interrupts your business. This could include lost income while your business is shut for repairs. Generally, the figures are based on your yearly income.

Ask for cover that guarantees you payment on a weekly basis for cash-flow purposes and not for payment at the end of a claim for repairs. Bills need to be paid regardless of an interruption to your business. Claim payments should be received until normal business can proceed and you have regained the income you would normally expect. These payments are based on last year's figures for the same time of year and not necessarily on your busiest period. Even when the work to repair or replace is complete, the claim payments should be on a descending scale until your business returns to normal.

Your building and contents insurance should reflect all the contents and the buildings independent of one another. Insurance is based on replacing and repairing, not on market value, so ask a builder or valuer to provide you with an estimate. Then add a percentage to this figure for the removal of debris, architect's fees (if applicable) and any other costs.

An insurance policy is a legal, binding contract with terms and conditions. Make sure that all the items you wish to insure are covered.

Discuss a workers' compensation policy with your insurer. It is advisable to have a personal accident and sickness/income policy.

Fraud and theft in the restaurant business

Look out for the following:

☐ Short-changing and overcharging.

☐ Issuing food without an order – complicity between kitchen and waiting staff.

☐ Deleting an order as a 'no sale' or cancelled order and pocketing the money.

☐ Stock sold for cash.

☐ Selling stock to other businesses.

☐ The use of stolen credit cards.

☐ Running off more than one transaction at a time for the same sale.

☐ Suppliers adding the date into the total, short-weighing and overcharging.

☐ Suppliers delivering short orders and charging for the complete order.

☐ The theft of food, drink, equipment and money by staff.

To combat this, some large restaurants are installing CCTV cameras over tills. Install automated till systems. Stocktake regularly. A foolproof system against fraud is not possible, so be vigilant.

CREDIT CARDS

In today's market, payment by card is the preferred method. Accepting credit cards brings the following benefits to your business:

☐ More customers through your door if they see that their card is accepted.

☐ No cash restrictions can mean that your customers spend more.

☐ An increased turnover and profit.

☐ Your banking becomes automated, making procedures simpler and faster.

Our increasingly cashless society demands the use of credit and debit cards in most restaurants, although some quick turnaround restaurants only work on cash because the costs charged by the card companies are too high.

Negotiate charges with the card companies and renegotiate those charges a year after trading. They may see a good, profitable company in the making and may wish to partake of your success in the long term.

LEGAL TIPS

Don't put your personal assets at risk

If you are starting a business with one or more people, you can choose partnership, limited liability partnership or limited company status. In a partnership all partners are jointly liable for debts. If you come up against a legal problem you will be risking your personal assets.

Putting it in writing

Put all your business deals and agreements in writing. If you have a verbal agreement, obtain confirmation in writing. A written record will also prevent people from trying to change their minds or giving you a different story at a later stage.

It pays to get advice early on

Get legal advice early on as this will pay in the long run. Problems can arise in the long term if this is neglected. Ask for an estimate of the cost if you seek a lawyer's advice. If you are forming a company, shop around for a solicitor's package deal.

Getting someone to recommend a solicitor

Solicitors specialise in many areas of the law and it may be difficult to find one who is right for your business. Recommendations from other companies are a good start. Ask solicitors for testimonials and references and follow these up.

Keeping up to date with changes in the law

Employment law is constantly changing, so keep up to date. Every employer must provide a statement of employment clearly laying down certain details. It can be in your interests to include policies that are not needed by law to safeguard yourself.

BUSINESS ADVICE ORGANISATIONS

Business Debtline

The hope is that good finance and accountancy practices have been adhered to from the start of your business plans, but there may be worrying times when some good, practical advice from experts would help enormously.

Contact Business Debtline (0800 197 6026), a national telephone service that offers free, confidential and independent advice to small businesses on tackling cash flow problems by:

- ☐ preparing a budget for your business;

- ☐ prioritising all your debts;

- ☐ dealing with court proceedings;

- ☐ understanding bankruptcy;

- ☐ avoiding the repossession of your home and business;

- ☐ dealing with tax matters; and

- ☐ negotiating with creditors and bailiffs and dealing with most other debt and cash-flow issues you and your business may face.

Federation of Small Businesses

The Federation of Small Businesses (FSB) is the leading organisation in the UK, and it campaigns to improve the financial and economic environment in which small businesses operate. Alongside this influential lobbying, FSB members also enjoy a unique protection and benefits package providing instant access to legal and professional advice and support.

For further details, visit their website: (www.fsb.org.uk).

Other organisations

There are government agencies and organisations that can help you make the right business decisions.

The Small Business Service (SBS) operates a number of schemes and initiatives that are designed to help small businesses in a variety of ways. They encourage businesses to be more innovative and to exploit new technologies, they help them obtain finance more readily and can provide ways for businesses to measure and improve their efficiency. Their website is www.business.link.gov.uk.

The SBS also oversees the work of the local Business Link offices that operate throughout England. Similar services are Business Gateway for Lowland Scotland, Business Information Source in Highland Scotland, Business Connect in Wales and the Local Economic Development Unit for Northern Ireland.

The Business Links provide independent and impartial advice, information and a range of services to help small firms and those starting up new businesses. Call Business Link on (0845) 600 9006.

The British Chamber of Commerce (BCC) is the national face of the UK's network of accredited Chambers of Commerce. It campaigns to reduce burdens on business and to create a more favourable business environment. For further help, go to the BCC's website (www.britishchambers.org.uk).

5

RUNNING A SAFE BUSINESS

Running a safe, hygienic business is one of the biggest tests a restaurateur has to face. This chapter covers the restaurant's food hygiene, staff handling of the food, adhering to strict hygiene standards and the premises themselves.

This chapter outlines the Food Safety Act, the Food Premises Regulations, food hygiene training, temperature controls, and foods that need chilling and those that don't. Various types of food poisoning are discussed, and there is also advice on staff hygiene, environmental health requirements and the visit by an inspector.

FOOD SAFETY REGULATIONS

Food Safety Act 1990

Under this Act you must not:

- ☐ sell food (or keep for sale) anything that is unfit for people to eat;

- ☐ cause food to be dangerous to health;

- ☐ sell food that is not what the customer is entitled to expect, in terms of content or quality; and

- ☐ describe or present food in a way that is false or misleading.

Food Premises (Registration) Regulations 1991

Under this Act you must:

- ☐ register your business at least 28 days before opening a new food business; and

- ☐ contact your local authority for the appropriate (and very straightforward) form. There is no charge.

Food Safety (General Food Hygiene) Regulations 1995

Food hygiene training:

☐ regulations made under the Food Safety Act require that all persons who handle open food in the course of a food business receive food hygiene training.

☐ short course levels are foundation, intermediate and advanced. Find out what courses are available from your local authority.

Food Safety (Temperature Control) Regulations 1995

This covers the following:

☐ The temperature at which certain foods must be kept.

☐ Which foods are exempt from specific temperature control.

☐ When the regulations permit flexibility.

In Scotland the regulations are slightly different from the rest of the UK but the principles are the same. Contact your local authority.

TOP TIP — how to books small business start-ups

Foods that need temperature control must be kept either:

HOT at or above 63 °C; or

COLD at or below 8 °C.

STORING FOOD

Foods that need chilling

Foods that need chilling include the following:

☐ Milk, yoghurt, cream, butter, foods with cream filling, dairy-based desserts and certain cheeses.

☐ Many cooked products until ready to eat cold or heated. This includes most foods containing eggs, meat, fish, dairy products, cereals, rice, pulses or vegetables and sandwich fillings containing these ingredients.

☐ Most smoked or cured products such as hams unless the curing method means the product is not perishable at room temperature.

☐ Prepared, ready-to-eat meals including vegetables, salad leaves, coleslaw and products containing mayonnaise.

☐ Pizzas with meat, fish or vegetables.

☐ Foods with 'use by' and 'keep refrigerated' labels.

Foods that don't need chilling

These include:

☐ some cured/smoked products;

☐ bakery goods; and

☐ canned and dried foods such as pickles, jams and sauces, though these do need chilling once opened.

Mail-order food

Mail-order food must not be transported at temperatures that could cause a health risk. Therefore food that needs chilling should be delivered by a chilled compartment vehicle or in suitable packaging.

Fridge storage and temperature control

Meat storage at the base of the fridge is the rule to adhere to. A full guide can be obtained from your local authority. The fridge temperature should be between 1ºC and 4ºC to stop bacteria from multiplying. Keep a thermometer in the fridge and record a diary of temperatures for health and safety inspection. Keep it on the door to remind your staff to check the temperature levels.

FOOD POISONING AND AVOIDING CONTAMINATION

As a restaurateur you and your staff should understand what causes food poisoning and how it can be avoided. It is vital that your restaurant is clean throughout. The kitchen is naturally the place where cleanliness is of paramount importance. The food you serve must be absolutely safe, and by strictly following hygiene and cross-contamination rules, you will achieved this.

Several micro-organisms are the most common causes of food poisoning. While these make for alarming reading, they are preventable.

Campylobactor

This is the most common food-poisoning bug in the UK. It is found in raw and undercooked poultry, red meat, unpasteurised milk and untreated water. Just a piece of undercooked chicken can cause severe illness.

Symptoms: gastroenteritis with fever, abdominal cramps and diarrhoea that is often bloody. Can be fatal.

Salmonella

This is the second most common food-poisoning organism. It can be found in eggs, raw meat, poultry, unpasteurised milk and yeast, and even in pasta, coconut and chocolate. Salmonella grows in food until the food is chilled. It is also passed easily from person to person by poor hygiene, such as not washing hands.

Symptoms: usually mild, with abdominal pain, diarrhoea and nausea but rarely vomiting.

Clostridium perfringens

The third most common bug and the least reported because the symptoms are vague. It is found in soil, sewage, animal manure and in the guts of animals and humans. Food cooked slowly in large quantities then left to stand for a long time is its breeding ground.

Symptoms: when taken in large numbers, the bacteria produce toxins which attack the gut lining, causing diarrhoea and acute abdominal pain.

Listeria

This food-poisoning organism is particularly dangerous to pregnant women, babies and the elderly. It is found in soft, mould-ripened cheeses, patés, unpasteurised milk and shellfish. Listeria resists heat, salt, nitrate and acidity better than many other micro-organisms.

Symptoms: fever, headache, nausea and vomiting. Can be fatal to the elderly, immune-impaired infants and developing foetuses.

Scrombotoxin

Although not strictly speaking a bug, this poison is produced by certain bacteria in oily fish which has been allowed to spoil through inadequate refrigeration. It causes a dramatic histamine reaction. Scrombotoxin is found in fresh and tinned mackerel, tuna and – very rarely – Swiss cheese.

Symptoms: tingling or burning in the mouth, a rash on the face or upper body, itching, sweating and headache with a drop in blood pressure, abdominal pain, diarrhoea and vomiting.

E.coli 0157

Most strains of E.coli are harmless but those producing the poison verocytoxin can cause severe illness, E.coli 0157 being one. It is found in farm animals and land contaminated with their faeces, and it is transmitted through undercooked minced beef (such as burgers) and raw, contaminated milk.

Symptoms: abdominal cramps and bloody diarrhoea. In serious cases kidney failure, severe anaemia, neurological problems and death.

Preventing food poisoning

To combat food poisoning, obtain good clear advice from your local authority health inspector. All the above are perfectly possible to prevent if you are aware of them and how they can be avoided. Poisonings by salmonella and campylobactor are, however, on the increase due to a lack of understanding by those handling food.

A lack of common sense also features in food poisoning. Leaving raw chicken out in a hot kitchen for four hours without covering it is asking for trouble. It should have been refrigerated, of course. Preparing a sandwich on a board that has just been used for cutting up raw duck breasts is very bad practice. Keeping a bottle of milk on a hot window ledge throughout the day will almost certainly result in mild discomfort or worse if drunk.

Heavy-duty plastic or polypropylene colour-coded chopping boards must be used in a commercial kitchen, and these should be thoroughly scrubbed in hot, soapy water and rinsed after use to avoid cross-contamination and food poisoning. Use an antibacterial spray with kitchen towel.

A well publicised case of food poisoning occurred at a wedding when the entire buffet was laid out in a hot marquee for over four hours while pictures were being taken of the happy couple.

If space is at a premium, you may have to rethink your menu and your ordering if some items cannot be refrigerated for any length of time.

Eggs

Eggs have been under scrutiny for many years. Health and safety guidelines suggest that raw or semi-cooked eggs may pose a salmonella food-poisoning problem. All recipes printed in newspapers, magazines and books carry a warning not to serve undercooked eggs to the elderly or women who are pregnant (also see food poisoning earlier in this chapter).

It is your decision, therefore, whether to serve eggs that aren't thoroughly cooked (for example, eggs Benedict, poached or lightly scrambled eggs and Hollandaise sauce).

If you do, you may wish to add a note on the menu saying that particular dishes contain lightly cooked or raw egg to inform your customers and to safeguard your interests.

STAFF HYGIENE

Staff must always wash their hands with soap and dry them with clean towels after using the toilet. Hand washing must also take place to avoid cross-contamination after handling raw poultry, for example. Even if your kitchen staff nip out to the restaurant to check on a booking, they must wash their hands before resuming work with food.

Your staff must be instructed in other personal hygiene matters: fingers touching the face, nose, ears, hair or other parts of the body while working is unacceptable because this can spread infection and micro-organisms. Wearing a hat is a sensible option for kitchen staff. Waiting staff must also wash their hands before starting work and must abide by the personal hygiene rules mentioned above.

Cloths

Dishcloths and other cloths are a prime means of spreading germs. Use non-woven dishcloths rather than sponges because these have fewer traps for germs. Sponges also hold a great deal of water where bacteria can thrive.

Never mop the floor with a cloth that is used for counter tops. Regularly disinfect cloths in bleach and dry them flat, not scrunched up. Throw them away after extensive use. Change tea towels and hand towels often.

ENVIRONMENTAL HEALTH

You should have talked to environmental health officers about the required standards when you were looking at premises to obtain a clear picture of the requirements. Some properties may not be at all suitable or may not fit the required standards.

Environmental health requirements

Restaurant kitchens take a physical hammering, and so the effort needed to promote the best standards of hygiene, cleanliness, stock care and food rotation is a constant one. Take your eye off the ball – and your staff – and you could end up with a big food-poisoning problem. Watch Gordon Ramsay's television programme *Kitchen Nightmares* to see how poorly run some restaurant kitchens can be, due either to laziness or a lack of knowledge.

The role of the environmental health officer

Environmental health officers (EHOs) from local councils enforce the laws and, although some in the trade view these laws as draconian and over-the-top, the system can't be avoided. Some of their requests are legally binding whereas others are not, but the officer's advice can be invaluable, particularly for those starting up in business or for those whose standards have slipped.

EHOs can, by law, turn up unannounced at all reasonable hours and proceed to inspect your restaurant's kitchen, toilets, storage space, the restaurant itself and your rubbish area. They may also visit as a result of a complaint.

Some of the many items they will inspect are lids and labels on containers, the use of the right chopping boards, the fridge and freezer temperatures. They will take a keen interest in the suitability and cleanliness of tiles, floor, walls and ceilings, storage, hand basins for staff, how raw and cooked meat are stored in the fridge, air circulation and vermin problems.

There are EHO horror stories: stoves with no knobs where the staff turned the gas on with pliers, dirty stale oil left in fryers and filthy fridges with no labelling on the containers. They have also discovered babies' soiled nappies in kitchens, mould and mice droppings behind equipment, fire doors propped open with unsealed rubbish, and cleaning fluids transferred to lemonade bottles.

EHO inspection

The following is what you can expect when your business is inspected:

☐ The inspector will show identification.

☐ A routine inspection will be carried out.

☐ You will be given feedback about identified hazards and guidance on how they can be avoided.

☐ You will also be given the reasons in writing for any action you are asked to take.

☐ Where there is an apparent breach of law, you will receive a statement of what that law is.

☐ You will be given a reasonable time to meet the statutory requirements unless there is an immediate risk to public health.

☐ You are entitled to be informed of the procedures for appealing against local authority action.

☐ Some premises are inspected every six months, others much less often.

The inspectors' powers:

☐ They can take samples and photographs and can inspect records.

☐ They may write informally to you to put right any problems they found.

☐ Where breaches of the law are identified that must be put right, they may serve you with an improvement order.

☐ They can detain or seize goods.

☐ In serious cases they may decide to recommend a prosecution.

☐ If there is an imminent health risk to consumers, inspectors can serve an emergency prohibition order backed up by the court which forbids the use of the premises or equipment.

If you disagree with the outcome, contact your local authority's head of environmental health or trading standards services to see if the matter can be resolved informally. If disagreement remains, contact your local councillor.

Contact your local authority or trade association if you think the law is being applied differently from other authorities. Ask about LACOTS (Local Authorities Co-ordinating Body on Food and Trading Standards).

You have the right of appeal to a magistrates' court against an improvement notice or a refusal by a local authority to lift an emergency prohibition order made earlier by the court. A magistrates' court must confirm the emergency closure of a business or the seizure of food. If the magistrates decide the premises have been shut down without proper reason or food has been wrongly seized or detained, you have a right to compensation.

Other considerations include:

☐ the past history of the offence;

☐ the seriousness of the offence;

☐ the inspectors' confidence in the restaurant's management;

☐ the consequences of non-compliance; and

☐ the operator/proprietor's attitude.

Your local authority will help if you need any advice on food safety. Trade associations and independent consultancy services can also help.

6

CHOOSING THE DESIGN AND EQUIPMENT

Careful design defines how functional the overall restaurant and kitchen will be. This chapter deals with the design of the hall, the bar and the restaurant itself. It will also help you with the choice of chairs and tables and gives tips on flooring, walls and ceilings, toilets and lighting and how to dress a restaurant table from top to toe.

It also discusses what to look out for in kitchen design and kitchen equipment, from a lemon squeezer to a fridge and stove. China, glass, cutlery and that all-important service from kitchen to restaurant and back again wrap the chapter up.

DESIGNING YOUR RESTAURANT

Restaurants can be described like this: the kitchen is the factory, and the restaurant is the sales office and showroom. Once you accept this approach, the better your planning and the outcome will be.

Restaurant design has changed considerably since the 1990s. Professional designers now mostly design with the 'wow factor' in mind, especially in corporate restaurant businesses. All that metal. All that 'leather' seating. All that minimalist lighting. To my mind, they all look the same.

But is it necessary to employ a professional designer to achieve a style or, more importantly, a friendly, smart environment that is pleasing to the eye? The restaurant's interior – and exterior – will convey to the public your taste, your style. So how do you go about it?

Professional design

Seek out some professional expertise before you leap into the unknown or visit restaurants to obtain some ideas of the traits you wish to incorporate. But beware of clashing styles or a cluttered look. An integrated overall style is best. Beware too of designs that do not focus on the customers' and staff's basic needs, such as comfort and the ability to move around to serve at tables. The look has to be in proportion to the space.

DIY design

Resist the urge to put up artefacts brought back from a holiday in Turkey and Mexico unless these fit into the overall design. Equally, resist the homey high-street chain store look because this will be instantly recognisable. Customers rarely want to sit in a restaurant that resembles their home – they can do this quite easily with a takeaway. These products may not be robust enough to withstand the hard wear and tear demanded in a public space, so visit a specialist restaurant furniture shop and commercial kitchen business.

A design will be most effective if it recognises its clientele. For example, pine tables and wooden chairs achieve a look that is inviting to many people, thanks to its approachability. This look says 'inexpensive meal out'. However, looks can be deceiving.

As a guide, allow 2¹/₂–4 square metres per person in the restaurant to take into consideration seating, table space, gangways and access to the bar/counter.

IS YOUR RESTAURANT FUNCTIONAL?

No matter how quirky or charming a restaurant is, it must first and foremost be *functional*. When investigating properties, look at the space from the point of view of it being full and working at full tilt. Now walk through the space from the restaurant's entrance to the back and note the following:

□ Is the shape of the property conducive to running a business? Or is the shape too awkward or the ceiling too low, thus creating huge noise levels?

□ Is there a flow for customers and staff to reach the tables comfortably? To get to the toilets? For staff to access the kitchen and bar?

□ What is the signage like outside and inside? Do these need improving?

□ Is the entrance welcoming, accommodating, well lit? Is the door handle user-friendly or do your customers have to fight to get in?

□ Is the entrance draught-free? Customers will not return if their table was in the direct line of a blast of cold air. A double-door lobby is one answer.

□ Where are the light switches for staff on entry? If you or they have to stumble around in the dark to turn the lights on, this could be hazardous.

□ Is there a good cloakroom area for coats, shopping bags and umbrellas? When full to bursting, will this area be another battleground for entry into the restaurant if it is located by the main entrance? If so, can you solve this problem by placing coats elsewhere (but not near tables as coats on pegs brushing against customers' heads are not acceptable)?

☐ Is there a large enough entry to take in deliveries? Or is there a good, accessible entry point at the back of the property?

Now make a list of any improvements you should make to the decoration, signage, lighting and flooring.

THE HALL AND BAR

Make your entrance welcoming and uncluttered so that the customer has easy access and so that you can see and greet the customer.

If you have the space, a bar is an invaluable area, not only for its instant appeal to drinkers on entering the restaurant, but also because it functions as a service area. It acts as a control for ordering, making bills out, housing the cash register, taking bookings, making phone calls to suppliers, a focal point for staff, a place to sit down when doing paperwork, storing paperwork and records, plus menu and wine list storage.

The bar may store a percentage of your wines and other drinks, plus glasses, ice, perhaps a glass washer and sink and other items for drinks service. Place racks at the back of the bar for wine storage. Keep this stocked up because it adds to presentation as well as being practical.

 Keep the bar as uncluttered as possible because this is the focal point of your restaurant. Also keep it spotless.

The bar is useful for drinks sales because it displays what you have on offer and may also house a coffee machine. Good coffee is now expected, and so you should invest in an espresso machine. These can be leased or bought. They add atmosphere as well as the promise of a well made cup of coffee, and they are also money-makers, as all the Caffe Nero's, Starbucks and others will testify to.

If you have no space for a bar you will need to find room elsewhere for making out bills, opening wine, storing menus and all that goes with the smooth running of a restaurant. But, of course, there are places that do not need a bar, such as the country-house restaurant or café.

LAYING OUT THE RESTAURANT

Tables

The flow is your mantra when you are designing any part of your restaurant. But first, what type is your restaurant: casual, formal, a quick lunch place, a big-spend restaurant? How much per head do you expect to make? These are crucial questions to ask as they determine your type of table, the space in between, the comfort of your chairs for a long or quick meal, where you place your bar and any service stations.

Do you go for round, square or rectangular tables seating two, four, six and eight? Tables with legs or pedestals? Interchangeable round tops? Obtain accurate measurements of tables and chairs from a variety of manufacturers and place markers or string around the restaurant before committing yourself to buying the furniture. It may not fit in and may be too bulky, making your restaurant look like a furniture showroom.

- ☐ 76-cm square tables seat two customers.
- ☐ 1-m square tables seat four.
- ☐ 1-m round tables seat four.
- ☐ 1.52-m round tables seat eight.
- ☐ 137 × 76 cm rectangular tables seat four.

If you have a designer it may be possible to have a graphic design or a scale model to experiment with.

Do you choose tables that don't require a tablecloth or ones that do? Put under-padding under tablecloths for extra luxury and to safeguard the surface.

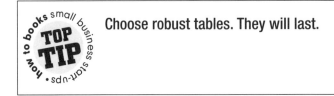 **Choose robust tables. They will last.**

Be flexible

The more flexible your seating, the more you will be able to offer individual requirements for parties. The whole restaurant may be booked by a single party, and you will need to know how many you can seat comfortably and with reasonable staff access to each seat. Obviously round tables can create problems with large parties because they can't be joined together. But you can buy tables with differing lift-off top sizes and shapes so that you can be as flexible as possible.

Flow paths must be maintained from kitchen to tables and from bar to tables. How accessible are the toilets?

Tables by the kitchen door are to be avoided at all costs. That swinging door nearby and a constant flow of staff and noise just aren't acceptable. Not for nothing is this table known in the trade as Siberia. Instead, use this inhospitable space for a service station that houses napkins, cutlery, bread, condiments, candle holders and other items of use for your staff to minimise their entry into the kitchen. This can be waist high with several shelves or a simple wooden table.

Chairs

The more formal the dining, the longer the customer will stay. The last thing you want is shifting, uncomfortable customers, so a well upholstered chair is essential.

Beware of high backs, arm rests and a bulky design if you have a small restaurant because these will take up valuable space. They must be practical if the whole restaurant is taken over for a party and they must fit the space.

Avoid making a costly mistake by choosing chairs for their aesthetic qualities. They may look elegant and smart, but are they up to the job of comfortably and securely holding the increasing girth of the nation? Can they withstand the wear and tear of a busy restaurant?

Points to consider:

  □ Either ask a manufacturer to come up with a style to suit your restaurant or choose chairs from the range of designs on the market.

  □ Customers rock backwards on their chairs, so choose a robust chair with splayed legs and a strong frame.

  □ Take a few sample chairs home with you to sit on over several days in your office and dining room to find the most comfortable one.

  □ Choose chairs that can stack so that you can store them without taking up too much room.

☐ For a more casual, quick turnaround restaurant, you will still need a chair that is reasonably comfortable and not one that catches your customers in the backs of their thighs, causing a lot of shifting.

☐ Most modern chairs are wood or a mixture of metal and wood, which can make a great deal of noise on a wooden floor. Ask the advice of the salesperson or manufacturer about how this can be overcome because it can be very distracting for other diners and causes wear and tear on your staff's nerves.

☐ Fixed seating, such as banquettes, is becoming increasingly popular but is inflexible. Benches in casual restaurants are also gaining in popularity thanks to our increasingly informal society.

☐ As a guide, a chair seat is usually 46 cm from the ground, and its depth from the front edge of the seat to the back of the chair is also 46 cm. The height from the ground to the top of the back is 1 metre.

Flooring, walls and ceilings

Wood is *the* chosen flooring for new and revamped restaurants. It looks smart, clean and light and is easy to maintain. The drawback is high noise levels when chairs are scraped on the floor when diners sit or leave. There also is no cushioning of other noises – voices, plates, cutlery, music – that would be soaked up by carpeting.

However, carpeting stains, absorbs smell, needs more cleaning and doesn't have the longevity of wooden flooring. It can also deaden noise and therefore lessen the character of a bustling, buzzing place. If you have several levels of floor space, however, you could have some carpet and some wood, which would accentuate the atmosphere.

Wallpaper is out, painted walls are in. Absorbent materials for the ceiling will help enormously in controlling noise. Beware of too low a ceiling, which will add to the heat and noise. Lighting and electrical points must be designed before decoration.

Consider having heating installed under the floor before laying flooring, and install ventilation (and air-conditioning too if this is your choice) before you tackle the ceiling.

Toilets

Toilets are often the last concern for many restaurateurs, who prefer to spend their money on other aspects of the business. But the British are aghast at poorly maintained loos and will often cross a restaurant off their list of where to eat out if this is the case.

However, a new breed of toilets is thankfully making its mark: smart stand-alone bowls, mixer taps, innovative glass panels, good-sized mirrors, ventilation and subdued, flattering lighting are just some recent design features. This shows respect for the customer, even if the customer doesn't reciprocate in quite the same way.

☐ Make sure that the signage to the toilets is clear.

☐ Designate staff to keep the toilets clean during opening hours. Nothing is more depressing than to enter toilets strewn with used paper towels, dirty sinks, loo paper on cubicle floors and overflowing bins. Have a weekly rota of staff to carry out checks before each service.

☐ Design the toilets for easy maintenance.

☐ Before service, make sure there is plenty of toilet paper in each cubicle.

☐ If the toilets are small don't install a hand dryer which will heat up the room to uncomfortable levels. Put in paper towels instead or an extending towel roller. Hand dryers add to the noise level and their efficiency is questionable. How often do you see fellow loo users wiping their hands on their clothes after using a dryer?

☐ Make sure all toilet cubicle locks work and are maintained.

☐ If the toilets are close to tables, make sure there is a door to the area that is self-closing and that doesn't squeak.

☐ Do the toilets smell sweet? If not, why not?

☐ Sadly, good toileteries – smart hand soaps, liquid soaps, tissue boxes, cotton wool for makeup removal – disappear. Go for toileteries that are attached to walls or don't offer anything except soap and towels unless you are in the luxury class and take into budgetary consideration these 'disappearances'.

☐ Avoid 'funny, ha ha' names such as Tou Louse as seen in an arty French eatery, Little Boys and Little Girls rooms and the like.

☐ Keep the toilets simple yet smart. But you could be bold with the décor. Add a bit of colour if your restaurant has muted shades.

Lighting

Lighting is one of the most important factors to get right. It adds atmosphere, a warming colour and tone, and makes the food even more appealing.

☐ Use dimmers to create instant atmosphere and mood, but don't make your restaurant too dark so that reading the menu, a wine list or paying the bill can become a trial rather than a pleasure.

☐ Lighting fixtures can be as decorative or unobtrusive as suits the décor.

☐ Avoid overhead lighting. This is very harsh. Small inset ceiling lighting can work if designed with skill. Side and uplighting is more flattering than overhead lighting.

☐ Table lamps can work in some instances, but beware of looking like a lighting showroom with too many table lamps squashed into a small area.

☐ Don't destroy the atmosphere by bright lighting coming in from halls or the kitchen. Each time the kitchen door opens it lets out a ray of (perhaps) fluorescent light, which can kill the mood.

☐ Exterior lighting needs to be welcoming. Light up the mandatory menu frame by the door so that the menu can be easily read by passing trade.

Dressing a table

Table spacing is of great importance, especially in a more formal restaurant. However, in a fast, casual restaurant, tables that are close together are more acceptable and can add atmosphere.

Table linen

Tablecloths and napkins are expensive to hire and launder. When done in-house without care they can look penny pinching if they are not starched or ironed properly. Cloths suit certain restaurants and not others: a bistro, café or wine bar may not need any. Factor the cost into the day-to-day expenses of running your restaurant to see if hiring linen is feasible. Obtain several quotes. Hire companies will also supply glass cloths and hand towels for the toilets.

White or cream is best for showing off food, glasses and flowers and to convey freshness and cleanliness. Dark cloths add gloom and don't help the food. The materials used for dark tablecloths are usually inferior to crisp white or cream linen.

If your restaurant is better suited to red-and-white check tablecloths to convey a pleasingly cheap and cheerful atmosphere, then follow your instincts. Or you may wish to follow the continental style with paper tablecloths or paper tablecloths over a cloth.

Tablecloth sizes:

- 137cm × 137cm to fit a table 76 cm square or a 1-metre round table.
- 183 cm × 183 cm to fit a table 1 metre square.
- 183 cm × 244 cm to fit rectangular tables.
- 183 cm × 137 cm to fit smaller rectangular tables.
- Slipcloths (to cover just the top of the tablecloth): 1 m × 1 m.
- Linen napkins: 46–50 cm square.
- Buffet tablecloths: 2 m × 4 m – minimum size.
- Tea and glass cloths: the best are linen or cotton.

Napkins should be simply folded in half. Gone are the days of showing off your staff's origami skills: they have better things to do with their time and skills. Nor should they be picked up and draped over the customer's lap. This is an unwarranted affectation and usually an embarrassment to the customer.

Flowers

If you are dressing your tables with flowers, there is no need for an entire bouquet because a single stemmed rose in a simple, clear glass vase will add class and colour. Tall flower arrangements should be avoided as customers may not be able to see one another – not what people come to restaurants for.

Cutlery

When buying cutlery, try it out to see how comfortable it is in your hands. Go for a simple, unfussy design that will not become dated. Buy quality because this won't tarnish. Your staff have enough to do without resorting to removing stains from cutlery before setting tables. There is no need for an armed phalanx of cutlery placed on the table. Cutlery for one course will do, with cutlery added depending on the ordered courses. Simplicity is best.

Glasses

Avoid the temptation of buying glasses for their looks alone because the shape and thinness of a glass can have a marked effect on wine. Thick Paris goblets are a big no-no. They may last for ever but don't do anything for wine. Go instead for a plain, clear glass with a good-sized bowl that tapers towards the rim so that your customers can swirl the wine around to release the aromas and flavours. Avoid overly huge balloon glasses which may denote largesse but which break easily and will cause your staff to have nervous breakdowns washing and drying them.

Always wash glasses immediately, then rinse them in hot water and dry. Before setting them on tables or putting them on shelves, re-wipe them with a clean cloth to remove any tinge of detergent – a sure-fire way of ruining wine.

Water glasses and other glasses should be the same design as the wine glasses for continuity and style.

Other items
Condiments should preferably be designed simply to avoid 'walking'. The more covetable the items, the more you will have to replace them. If you are using the currently trendy salt and pepper mills, make sure they are of decent quality (i.e. they do their job properly) or else they will need to be replaced at a cost to your profits.

Candles are here to stay. Just make them user-friendly – i.e. not tall, precarious ones that can be knocked over or that get in the way of service.

Depending on your type of restaurant consider marketing on your tables. Put menus, special deals, promotions and events on takeaway cards on the tables (but don't clutter or oversell) and some at strategic points around the restaurant.

LAYING OUT THE KITCHEN

The hub of the restaurant has to work efficiently. Restaurants can fail as a result of a poorly designed kitchen, so it is important to consult with a professional if you are new to the restaurant business. Ask a commercial kitchen equipment company for their advice. You may be taking over a premises that already has some equipment and adding other equipment to upgrade the kitchen. Or you may be starting from scratch. Involve the chef, your partners, the builder, plumber, carpenter and architect in these crucial discussions, be it an upgrade or a whole new kitchen.

A restaurant kitchen is divided into:

☐ prepping area;

☐ cooking area;

☐ washing-up area; and

☐ service.

Storage takes place in all four areas.

A smaller kitchen operation may have to compromise on space, while larger kitchens will have the following prepping areas to function at speed:

- ☐ vegetables;

- ☐ fish;

- ☐ poultry;

- ☐ meat;

- ☐ desserts.

Contrary to popular belief, it is not necessary to have a huge kitchen to operate well. A galley kitchen can work excellently for a small restaurant because little walking is involved and everything is to hand, apart from perhaps the storage, fridges and freezer which will be nearby. A further excellent advantage is that the kitchen is constantly being cleaned as the chef(s) cook. The chef establishes a good rhythm.

Kitchen needs

Your first consideration is what you expect your kitchen to achieve. What kind of food will you be putting on the menu? The menu will dictate what kind of equipment you need and where it should be placed for efficiency and practicality. What can the kitchen handle?

It's not how much a kitchen costs but what you do with it. What is your budget? Will future chefs the proprietor takes on be able to adapt to the kitchen set up by the current chef? Basics, such as good knives, a solid cooker, a large refrigerator and good storage space are prerequisites, so chefs must – and do – adapt.

Consult *Yellow Pages* for catering companies that supply the large equipment, pots and pans, clothing and knives. Your library will have London and other large towns' *Yellow Pages* (or go on the web). Or ask a restaurateur or two for personal recommendations.

Kitchen flow

After deciding on the type of food, the kitchen flow is your next consideration: flow for deliveries to storage spaces, the flow of prepared food to service, the flow to the dining room and dirty dishes from the dining room, plus the flow of waiting staff *vs* kitchen staff in the kitchen. Rarely should they meet physically in the kitchen.

For example, if waiting staff are responsible for the bread, butter and other peripherals, these must be accessible at some point in the kitchen or at a service station in the restaurant where they won't stop the chefs in their tracks.

Kitchen legislation

Consult your local environmental health officer prior to working on your kitchen to ensure that all the necessary steps are taken to abide by the legislation (see Chapters 3 and 5).

Kitchen equipment

The basic kitchen requirements are as follows:

□ A double oven with four or six gas burners and a solid top (a solid piece of metal that covers the whole stove, the burner underneath spreading heat all around for keeping items warm or for cooking when turned up).

□ A grill or salamander (high-level grill).

□ A deep-fat fryer.

□ A large commercial fridge or a walk-in fridge.

□ A freezer.

□ A double sink.

□ A hand basin.

□ A sink, preferably near the cooking area.

□ A washing-up area with a commercial dishwasher and storage shelving.

□ A hot plate with infra-red lamps if space and money allow (I found it invaluable in my restaurant kitchen) for plating up and situated where waiting staff can easily access it.

□ A cool work surface for cold food, pastry and salad prep away from the ovens.

☐ Work surfaces for prepping food and surfaces for food processors, for example.

☐ Hanging pot and pan racks to increase storage space, preferably by the stoves.

☐ Good, accessible storage for cooking equipment, glasses, cutlery, serving dishes, plates, etc. Time and motion studies should be worked out: plates near the plating area, coffee cups by the coffee prep area.

☐ A rack for food orders placed in order taken.

☐ Good lighting and decent air flow.

☐ A telephone.

If you are using a microwave, make a space for it. Other equipment you could consider includes a steamer, a griddle, a convection oven for pastry, a professional ice-cream maker, other refrigeration and freezers.

Other spaces are required for the following:

☐ Cool vegetable and fruit produce storage area away from heat.

☐ Dry-goods storage away from heat.

☐ Non-food storage for linen.

☐ Non-food storage for cleaning materials, buckets, mops, light bulbs, toilet paper, refuse bags and vacuum cleaner.

☐ Alcohol storage.

☐ Rubbish.

☐ An office for paperwork. Don't underestimate the amount of paperwork! If no space is available, try to find a permanent spot to store it and process the paperwork in the restaurant when it is closed.

☐ Storage for staff belongings.

Buying equipment

Look for good, solid equipment on castors for easy cleaning and consider second-hand equipment for cutting down the cost of your kitchen. But buy sensibly, not just because it's a bargain. It may not be a few months down the line.

The restaurant you are taking over may have suitable equipment included in the price. If so, make sure all is in working order, establish who services the equipment, obtain any attached paperwork from the seller and insist that it is cleaned thoroughly before you take over the property.

If you are buying from specialists, ask for training to be given to the kitchen staff who will use it.

Always install a commercial dishwasher. This takes a fraction of the time of a domestic one and the interior is designed without frills to fit in the maximum amount of dishes or pots and pans. There is usually a separate tray for glass washing.

The following is a checklist of cooking equipment to fill those shelves:

☐ Heavy-duty, cast-iron frying pans.

☐ Sauté pans, shallow pans, Dutch ovens (for braising, sauteing or stews).

☐ A pancake pan.

☐ A steamer.

☐ Cast iron casseroles with lids.

☐ A fish pan.

☐ Heavy-based stock pots.

☐ Heavy-based saucepans for sauces, etc.

☐ Knives for many uses – only buy good quality; these will last a lifetime (see page 74).

☐ Chopping boards.

☐ Plastic-lidded containers for food storage and labels.

☐ Mixing bowls of all sizes.

☐ Measuring jugs.

☐ Kitchen scales.

☐ Whisks.

☐ Ladles.

☐ Large spoons.

☐ Slotted spoons.

☐ Kitchen scissors.

☐ Sieves and colanders.

☐ A chinois (fine sieve).

☐ Graters.

☐ Terrines, ramekin dishes.

☐ Roasting and baking trays.

☐ Pastry brushes.

☐ Spatulas.

☐ A lemon squeezer.

☐ A nutmeg grater.

☐ A fish slice.

☐ A pepper and a salt mill.

☐ An apple corer.

☐ A funnel.

☐ A corkscrew.

☐ A lemon zester.

☐ A mandoline.

☐ A cheese grater.

☐ Anything else that is suited to your menu.

Knives

It never pays to buy cheap knives. Look out for Gustav, Emil & Ern, Sabatier, Sheffield Steel, Victorinox, Ed. Wustof and my favourite, J. A. Henkels.

I still have cherished knives from my 1980s restaurant days which, despite the outlay, are in excellent condition and are as effective as the day they were bought. Chefs will provide their own sets, which have been built up over their careers.

The basics:

☐ A large chopping knife.

☐ A sharpening steel or an electric/water sharpener.

☐ A palette knife.

☐ A carving knife.

☐ A chef's knife – 15 cm.

☐ A medium knife – 20–25 cm.

☐ A filleting knife (for fish).

☐ Several paring knives (such as a vegetable knife).

☐ A potato peeler.

☐ A meat cleaver.

☐ A ham slicer with a supple blade.

☐ A boning knife.

☐ A salmon knife.

☐ A bread knife.

☐ A cheese knife.

☐ A cooking fork.

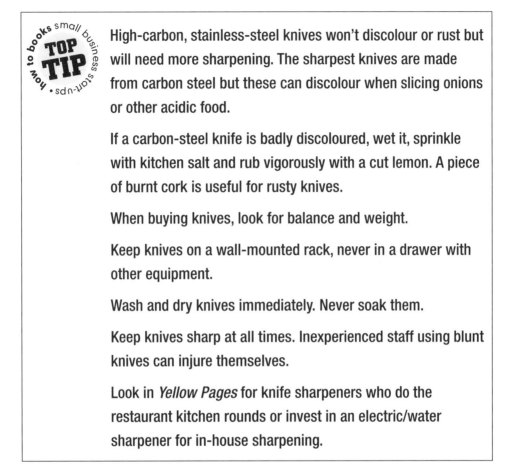

High-carbon, stainless-steel knives won't discolour or rust but will need more sharpening. The sharpest knives are made from carbon steel but these can discolour when slicing onions or other acidic food.

If a carbon-steel knife is badly discoloured, wet it, sprinkle with kitchen salt and rub vigorously with a cut lemon. A piece of burnt cork is useful for rusty knives.

When buying knives, look for balance and weight.

Keep knives on a wall-mounted rack, never in a drawer with other equipment.

Wash and dry knives immediately. Never soak them.

Keep knives sharp at all times. Inexperienced staff using blunt knives can injure themselves.

Look in *Yellow Pages* for knife sharpeners who do the restaurant kitchen rounds or invest in an electric/water sharpener for in-house sharpening.

BUYING CHINA AND TABLEWARE

Depending on the style of your restaurant, the alternatives are *bone china*, which may be chosen by a no expense-spared restaurant, or *earthenware*, the most popular because of its strength and affordability. *Stoneware*, a natural ceramic, durable finish which is more costly than earthenware, may suit small, casual restaurants.

White or cream tableware shows off food to its best advantage and also blends in with every conceivable décor. Patterned china can become dated and tiresome if the design is too busy, and it may also be difficult to replace in the long-term. Your best bet is therefore plain china. But don't see this as limiting because shapes, sizes and a coloured rim can all add a touch of class if this is what you are seeking.

Look, however, for durability and rolled edges that can withstand lots of handling and washing. Is the make dishwasher-proof and is there a guarantee from the manufacturers that the chosen china will be around for many years to come to replace broken, chipped or 'gone-walking' items?

If you are choosing super-sized plates, large soup bowls or rectangular-shaped plates, bear in mind the strength of your waiting staff's wrists and the extra miles they may have to walk if only two plates can be carried at one time. Will those varied, angular designs be more prone to chipping? Will fewer fit into your dishwasher at one time, thereby bumping up the cost of cleaning if more washes are done?

A rule of thumb for the amounts of china to invest in per restaurant cover is as follows:

- ☐ Four small plates.

- ☐ Four medium-sized plates.

- ☐ Two large plates.

- ☐ Two soup plates or bowls.

- ☐ Two cups and saucers.

- ☐ Four serving dishes (if plating main courses and serving vegetables or salads separately).

- ☐ One and a half butter dishes, milk jugs, sugar bowls, tea and coffee pots.

But before investing in china and taking that rule of thumb as gospel, consider the following:

- ☐ The type of menu on offer.

- ☐ The maximum and average seating capacity.

- ☐ The rush hour turn-over.

- ☐ The washing up facilities and turn-over.

Underplates

For more upmarket restaurants, underplates are still used for improving the presentation (or ostentation, depending on your point of view) and for carrying soup plates or bowls. They are also employed to ease the carrying of hot items and for carrying cutlery alongside the dish being transferred from one place to another. Doilies are past their sell-by date, but a napkin (paper or otherwise) can help a non-slipping bowl to arrive at its destination on an underplate.

Presentation plates are common in Michelin star restaurants and other similarly expensive restaurants, where they add an extra plushness to the meal. These are often gold-rimmed, strikingly patterned plates that are then whisked away before the customer can even add a fingerprint. The choice is yours, but I suspect they make the average diner feel a little uncomfortable.

 When storing and stacking china, don't go for the Great Wall of China but, instead, a mini one of no more than 24 plates to prevent a Great Fall.

Cutlery

Thankfully, the banks of cutlery that can be so off-putting for diners unused to many courses have been mainly phased out. There is no need to buy soup spoons, for example, because dessert and soup spoons can perform the same task. Some may, however, disagree. Fork and knife sizes can be the same, so there is no need to buy differing sizes. But you may still need a butter knife which should preferably be small to balance on a side plate. This can double up as a cheese knife.

In today's eating-out society, forget pastry forks, sugar tongs, grapefruit spoons, asparagus holders and curved-point cheese knives. They belong, thankfully, to the dainty past.

Stainless steel or silver plate? Which will you choose? Before deciding, look at plain patterns and cutlery that will last and not stain. Obtain a guarantee from the manufacturer for its lifespan, clean it well and store your cutlery with care to help to prolong its life.

Plainly designed cutlery, like china, will not date and will clean more easily and be more hygienic. But do choose it after selecting your china. It has to complement the china and add to the style of your restaurant.

Stainless steel is available in a variety of grades and is finished by different degrees of polishing: high polish, dull polish and a light matt. Silver plate has two grades: standard for general use and restaurant thicker grade.

Store your cutlery in individual drawers or spaces at a convenient height for your staff. Long, rectangular baskets in more casual restaurants are quite common. When drying cutlery, place it on a tray to carry it to the storage space to reduce handling. Make sure that all cutlery, when placed on the tables, is clean and untarnished.

ORGANISING THE SERVICE

As mentioned previously, it is important to get service right, with flow from the kitchen to the restaurant and vice versa. When waiting staff come in with the order or leave with the food, it is preferable that they do so with as little disturbance as possible. So the collection point should be as near to the door as possible.

Where plates and other dirty items will be cleared to also needs to be considered to achieve a smooth-running kitchen and restaurant. Possible solutions include the following:

☐ Arrange the orders in order of receipt on the check rack and remove them when the order has left.

☐ Plated food should be placed on the hot plate under the infra-red lights prior to being taken to the restaurant so that it can be kept warm before staff arrive to deliver the completed dish. (This is known as the pass.)

☐ Position stacks of plates on a warmer or in a warming oven close to the ovens for plating up – or on a shelf above the warming plate.

☐ Cold food should be removed from refrigeration in good time for it to come close to, or be at, room temperature so that the food actually tastes how it should rather than be diminished by the cold.

☐ Cheese especially is poorly served if not brought to room temperature before service.

☐ Position the washing-up area and plate-clearing so that they don't encroach on the cooking and prepping area. From a hygiene point of view, it is important that these areas are separate and designed so that they are kept out of the way of the cooking staff.

Don't forget to improve your restaurant and to upgrade the menu and service. Your regular customers will like to see the place they know and love well maintained and improved from time to time.

7

MARKETING YOUR BUSINESS

Marketing is one of the most important aspects of your business, and it pays to keep on examining your marketing strategies while running your restaurant and to keep on re-evaluating your strengths – and weaknesses. As the restaurant market is such a varied one, you should demonstrate what kind of an establishment you are running so that you do not send out mixed messages. A clear, concise message to potential and existing customers is your goal.

The market is steadily becoming more sophisticated and the number of good restaurants to choose from is increasing considerably. It therefore isn't enough to sit back and think that your good cooking and beautifully situated, attractive restaurant will pull in the customers without some extensive marketing on your part. This is where the first-time restaurateur can become unstuck. *Work out a strategy, allocate funding and do your homework.*

 The restaurateur isn't the sole salesperson: your front-of-house staff are equally important, so involve them in getting your message across to customers. Get the customers in by marketing and continue the process once they're in. Subtlety is the key for the latter part of the operation: a big sell is a big turnoff.

This chapter covers:

☐ choosing a name;

☐ advice on signage to attract customers;

☐ your business cards and stationery;

☐ menu design; and

☐ the Internet.

In short, your promotional material. It also discusses the difficult question of advertising and how to launch yourself on to the market. It gives tips on obtaining a media profile and the importance of getting into the guides that matter. It gives constructive advice on dealing with critics and examines the possible expansion of your business via various routes, including cookery classes, corporate lunches and cookbooks.

The Business Link or Chamber of Commerce in your area may help you with some of your marketing needs. The costs vary, but a well devised, professionally prepared marketing strategy can be an obvious financial advantage.

FINDING YOUR TARGET MARKET

First, you should identify your initial target market:

1. **Your customers**: age, income, occupation, local businesses.

2. **Your customers' needs**: business lunches, outside catering, Sunday evening openings which may be an untapped market.

3. **The competition**: what attracts customers to other restaurants? What are their strengths, their market share? Is there a reason why there are few restaurants in the area?

4. **Trends**: changes in local tourism, lifestyle changes, population shifts.

How to obtain this information:

□ from the business section of your local library;

□ from tourism authorities;

□ from your local Business Link office;

□ from local commerce or traders' groups;

□ from professional market-research services; and

□ by talking to prospective customers, restaurant staff and suppliers.

CHOOSING YOUR RESTAURANT'S NAME

The name you choose is all important in attracting the right type of customer: do you see your business as a neighbourhood restaurant, a potential crowd-puller from afar, a brasserie or bistro, an ethnic restaurant, a gastro pub or café? Avoid gimmicky names if you want to create a reputation as being a good restaurant serving quality food and offering good service.

Consider what messages you would be sending out with rather questionable names such as Kitch 'n D'Or, Bizarre Bazaar, Thai Tanic, Cup 'O' Chino and Kwizeen. Depending on your market, you could go for a name that incurs a wry smile or choose one that fits your aims and personality.

Do not choose a name that is so bland no one remembers it or a complicated, tongue-twisting one your staff have to use to answer the phone. This vital marketing tool will also be affected if your customers can't pronounce the name to pass it on to their friends and colleagues.

Obviously, choosing a French or Italian name will pigeonhole you. Potential customers may possibly be put off by the narrow menu it may suggest. Your menu may start off in a French or Italian vein but if you branch out into Thai, Bangladeshi or fusion cooking of any global kind, passing trade – and customers who haven't been for a while – will not get that broader message. They may walk on, perhaps not wishing to choose from an entirely French or Italian menu without realising the treasure trove of dishes available. Alternatively, you may want to specialise in a certain type of cuisine by offering the best Italian or French food in your area and by keeping your menu resolutely to this type of food.

Should you be fortunate enough to have a property by a river, capitalise on this by calling it *The Restaurant on the Bridge* or an equivalent. This will draw people to you who read the guides, write-ups and advertising and who are always on the lookout for a restaurant with a good view. But name it appropriately and only if there *is* a view of the water: a feeling of being had won't win new customers. Finally, avoid clichéd names.

SIGNAGE

Your signage will have a huge impact on your business if you rely on passing trade or if new customers are to find your restaurant.

☐ First impressions count.

☐ Employ a professional sign-maker. Don't make your own signs unless you have the gift.

☐ Choose an unfussy, readable font.

☐ Match the design and font to your other promotional material.

☐ Match the sign to your building. If it's modern, be modern. If it's Georgian, avoid the Gothic. Keep it simple.

□ Add the street number in lettering large enough to be seen by a passing car.

□ Light the signs.

□ If you come across a sign in your area which appeals to you, find out from the business who the sign-maker is and contact them.

□ If you have a gate, fence or wall by the entry to your premises and you use any of these to place your signs on, make sure that bushes don't obstruct the signs.

□ Consider carefully the sign's colour and lettering for impact and legibility. One poorly made sign in my area in dark red with black lettering is illegible: the business has shot itself in the foot even before opening its doors.

□ Will your business benefit from several signs for customers approaching from more than one direction?

□ Contact your local authority for permission for signage and lighting prior to having the sign made. It may not be passed due to its size, colour or lighting, so play safe.

□ Signage within your premises may also be necessary (see Chapter 3).

Contact your local authority for any brown tourism signs you may be entitled to. This signage can have a good effect on your business.

PROMOTIONAL MATERIAL

Promotional material includes:

□ business cards;

□ printed paper;

□ flyers;

□ menus;

□ sample menus to take away;

□ newsletters; and

□ web pages.

Depending on the type and size of your business, you may not want or need all the above, but some will be essential. A small restaurant may only need business cards and may make its own menus and headed paper on a computer. Or a clearly written menu board may be your choice.

Choose the font very carefully: a funky, angular one will be difficult to read whereas a clean, clear one will show respect for your customers. Use the same font for all your promotional material.

Business cards

Include on your business cards your restaurant's name, address, complete telephone number, website, days of opening and times, strengths (fresh local fish, sea views, log fires, in the *Good Food Guide*) and a map on the back if your location is difficult to find. Also include your logo if you have one.

Keep it simple yet as informative as possible. Make your business cards stand out from the rest.

Stationery

Printed stationery (letterheads, invoices, etc.) should have a heading, your registered office (if applicable), address, telephone/fax, email, website and logo.

Compliment slips are useful for sending menus or for confirming a booking or other information by post. Position the 'with compliments' so that you are not forced to write all round it.

Publicity

Flyers
Flyers are useful for leaving information at various places and for handing out to passers-by. Include all the relevant information (where, what, when open) plus a sample menu and bullet points of your strengths. These can be A5 or compliment-slip size.

Brochures
Brochures are increasingly being employed as a market tool by upmarket restaurants. Include photographs, sample menus, opening times, a map, private dining facilities, car-park facilities, outside dining and the bar area. Avoid photographs of smiling people gazing at one another over a perfectly groomed table. You will want your restaurant to look its best, but you don't want to alienate people by inferring only 'perfect' people or a young crowd eat there.

Newsletters
Newsletters can be an invaluable to small restaurants, keeping regular customers informed of local and calendar events with suggestions of menus to match the event or time of year. They may also describe a special menu that ties in with a tight schedule, menu changes, new produce, a range of wines

new to the list or a celebration of the first year of opening. They can be as personal or restrained as befits your market and will help to keep your business in your customers' thoughts. Results often follow a mailing.

Menus

Menus are best kept simple, with the name of your restaurant as the heading. Use printed ones if your menu varies little or seasonally, or clearly hand-written or computer-printed ones if your menu is small and changes daily.

Thanks to computers, it is easy to create your menus and to print these when needed. Check them constantly and discard those that are at all marked. The covers for menus or wine lists must also be kept scrupulously clean and unmarked. A messy menu immediately gives the wrong impression and may indicate a less than sparkling kitchen.

Sample menus are an excellent marketing device. Don't forget to put the name of your restaurant and other relevant information on these slips. Make sure these sample menus, flyers and business cards are accessible and replenish the stocks regularly.

The Internet

A website is now a necessity for all types of businesses. They are relatively cheap and thus a vital marketing tool for small businesses which have a minimal marketing budget. Research other people's websites and either design yours yourself or employ a designer whose work appeals to you. Ask about the success of the designer's work (i.e. how many hits their websites attract). Look at a variety of websites for design inspiration. Obtain several quotes before committing yourself. Choose the background colour with care so that your website is readable. Some designers can be too ambitious so that the site is slow to load or difficult to read.

At the very least, include times and days of opening, how to book a table, sample menu and wine list, a map and a good photograph of the restaurant's exterior (if it merits it) and interior. If you want to be more ambitious, you could include a virtual tour of your premises.

Keep your website updated. Either do this yourself or agree on a monthly/ retainer fee with the web designer. Above all, keep it simple and easily navigable. A static website (i.e. one which doesn't change or update) can send out the wrong signals and can arguably be worse than no website at all. Don't do as some restaurateurs do to make themselves look up to date and add a website address to your promotional material, which, when you visit it, contains nothing. This gives off bad signals.

 **Put yourself in the shoes of a potential customer. Check that your website is welcoming, practical, professional looking and geared towards the customers whom you would like to attract.**

Customers now look to the Internet for information. In 2009, an estimated 73 per cent of UK households used the Internet. Traffic to your site is dependent on not only the website address on your promotional materials but also on search engines. Searchers may key in one specific word or a group of words, such as 'restaurants in Norwich'. Make sure the words a searcher is likely to use appear at the beginning and frequently throughout your website.

ADVERTISING

If you look through your local paper you will see the same restaurants' ads again and again. Christmas, Mothering Sunday and bank holidays bring out a rash of ads, from low to middle-range or chain restaurants but rarely from those that aim to offer top-quality food and service. These ads tend to offer meal deals with kids' food at vastly reduced prices.

In my experience as a restaurateur of a small, independent upmarket country restaurant, it simply doesn't pay to advertise. It is far more effective to use other marketing skills to get your message across: via the Internet. *Yellow Pages*, media relationships, guide books, mail shots, a newsletter, handouts and local tourism publications. Word of mouth is one of your most effective marketing tools. It has been estimated that every one satisfied customer will, in turn, tell between five and ten other people of their experience.

Targetting the audience

Should you decide to advertise, look carefully at the many local newspapers in your area to see if you are targetting the right audience. You can obtain a media blueprint from your local newspapers that which will give you a great deal of research information, but make sure this is up to date. Go to www.jicreg.co.uk (Joint Industry Committee for Regional Press Research) to find out about the readership statistics of the majority of UK newspapers.

When contacting the advertising department, ask pertinent questions about the following:

☐ The circulation.

☐ The readership: age groups and standard socioeconomic categories:

- A = higher managerial, administrative or professional.

- B = intermediate managerial, administrative or professional.

- C1 = junior managerial, administrative or professional.

- C2 = skilled manual workers.

- D = semi and unskilled manual workers.

- E = those in the lowest socioeconomic category.

☐ Shopping patterns: taking holidays abroad, buying new cars, etc.

☐ Paid-for or free newspapers.

☐ The best day to place an ad if a daily paper. Your ad might well be best placed on the entertainment page, which only comes out on Thursdays.

☐ The best section. Always stipulate where you would like your ad to be placed and, if it appears on an inappropriate page, ask for it to be reprinted at no charge.

Ask for a copy of your ad so that you can proof-read it thoroughly. Look at local magazines and ask the same questions.

Other ways of advertising
These include paid for and free:

☐ *Yellow Pages.*

☐ Posters.

☐ Local tourism publications.

☐ Local Tourist Information offices or Visitor Information Service websites which may have an eating-out list.

☐ Direct mail.

☐ Newsletters for promotions, seasonal information, menus, staff changes.

☐ The Internet (look at your area for online restaurant sites).

Advertorials

An advertorial is a combination of public relations and ads. You agree to place a set number of ads in a newspaper and, in return, you receive a glowing report of your restaurant written by you and the advertising department. You will be persuaded to take out a series of ads, the argument being that it isn't worth your while having just one.

The advertorial may include a visit to your restaurant by a member of the newspaper's staff for a meal. The style of the place – virtually the entire menu, the wine list and character of mine host – will be given a 100-per-cent thumbs up. This fools no one and is seen as a very cheesy way of going about your business. Advertorials are best avoided if you are aiming at a good, discerning clientele.

Advertising nationally/internationally

Consider advertising in specialist interest magazines if, for example, your restaurant is in an area of outstanding natural beauty or an architecturally attractive city. Go to your library and look up the following publication guides:

- *Willings.*

- *Benn's Media Guide.*

- *BRAD (British Rate and Data).*

These will tell you what publications are on the market, their approximate advertising costs and how to contact them.

Other possibilities are to place ads in brochures and programmes allied to sporting events, such as Glorious Goodwood in Sussex. Go to your local Tourist Information office to research brochures and programmes for festivals, theatres, art galleries and art house cinemas to gauge their advertising possibilities.

Advertising wording

Your advertisement is selling your business so it must:

- grab the reader's attention;

- stimulate interest;

- plant the idea firmly in the reader's head that this may be the place for them and that they should act promptly;

□ be concise and give out the appropriate information – who you are, where you are, what you are offering, how you can be contacted, why they should book and when you are open; and

□ if your restaurant is in the *Good Food Guide* or any of the better guides, include this information.

Don't:

□ be pushy, arrogant or personal;

□ brag;

□ use flowery language; and

□ contravene the Trades Descriptions Act by offering something you can't deliver.

Other advertising tips

If you have taken over an existing business, there may already be an advertising contract. Re-evaluate this. When people book, ask them how they heard about your restaurant and use this information to help you gauge the effectiveness of the advertising – or is it a word-of-mouth booking?

Don't over-react to a cold call from a salesperson offering advertising. They will always try to persuade you with a must-have special offer or deal. Either ignore the call as politely as possible or ask them to send you details and then check the publication to see if the expense is worthwhile.

Stick to your budget.

Other marketing tips

If you plan to offer a discounted or good-value lunch, target retirement homes and sheltered-housing schemes. Distribute menus and flyers or leave these in the lobbies if permitted, or in the lobbies of community centres and other places that retired people may visit. Lunch is a booming part of business as more and more retired people prefer to dine out and drive/walk home in the daylight.

Leave a form on your tables for collecting names and addresses from your customers. Or enclose one with the bill so that you can remind them of your restaurant via a mail shot.

Make sure you put your restaurant's phone number and address in *Yellow Pages* and in the telephone directory. You can, of course, put an ad in *Yellow Pages* as well.

CREATING YOUR MEDIA PROFILE

Before you can decide how to attract the media you must first establish your unique strengths and what you are offering the public – and the media whom you would like to woo. Consider what your style is. Is it purely culinary? Mainly looks? Based just on the character of the owner and/or chef? Ideally it's a mix of all three. Independent restaurateurs must find their own voice, their own style to project, to sell to the media.

Free advertising – for this is what you will achieve by having a media presence – must be convincing, otherwise you are treading on dangerous ground when you are visited by the guides and critics. If it is all hype and no substance, the damage to your business by a bad review may be substantial.

Before toting for new business via media coverage, you must believe in yourself and be committed to being able to offer what you say you can offer. Can you deliver the goods? Think about what makes you unique and makes people want to come through your door.

Don't latch on to other people's styles. You should be true to yourself, otherwise your restaurant may look self-conscious, out of synch and out of place.

Media coverage: whom to target

Try to target:

□ local and national media;

□ restaurant reviewers, both local and national; and

□ restaurant guides.

How to achieve media coverage

Achieve media coverage through the personalities who work for you and through what is special about your restaurant:

□ A high-profile chef you have just taken on or one with an interesting pedigree or background.

□ A sommelier who knows their business and who has worked in a high-profile place or has an unusual background.

□ Your produce – perhaps it's unusual or sourced via an unusual producer.

□ Your building if it is historic, renovated to a high standard or on an interesting site.

☐ If you have changed from being a city high-flyer or a nun, or if you are the first Alaskan to open a restaurant in the area.

☐ Has your restaurant changed ownerships after twenty or so years in the hands of a much-loved local personality?

This is all newsworthy.

Research

Research your area's newspapers, magazines, radio and television. Ask for help at your local library about the publications available. Also consider reading/buying *the Guardian Media Guide* and looking up publications in *Willings* and *Benn's*.

Compile a media list of local and national newspapers, magazines, radio programmes and trade magazines, with contact numbers and email adresses.

When writing to a newspaper or magazine, phone first to find out whom to contact. Write down the correct spelling of this person's name and send them a press release (see below on how to write one) with a photograph of your restaurant's interior, your chef, a dish and the new owner. A picture tells a thousand words. But only do this if your budget can stand the cost of such an exercise. It is a waste of time and money if you don't find out exactly whom to target because your press release will simply be thrown away out and not forwarded to the right person.

Journalists are incredibly busy and some find it a distinct irritant to be called on the telephone. Others don't. If you do decide to throw caution to the wind, call them within a week or ten days of sending the release to establish first-hand contact.

Contact radio programme presenters (those who do interviews or have a magazine-style programme) to see if you can be interviewed, again having sent a press release and some background about your business to spark an interest.

It pays to keep your media list up to date and to send a press release on a regular basis to keep your business in their focus. But do not send non-newsworthy items because these they will go straight in the bin – or, worse still, you will be seen as a nuisance. Keep it professional, short and newsworthy.

Press releases

Press releases are an excellent tool for business promotion if they are properly written and presented. They are not a page-long ad and neither are they a promotional piece full of detail.

One common error is not to read the publication you are targeting before sending the press release. Do some homework: visit their website and look at the style, the content and, if possible, buy the publication. As a result, you will be able to understand the readers' expectations and will obtain a better response from your press release.

The golden rules for writing press releases:

☐ If sending by post, use headed paper with a contact name, address, phone, email.

☐ Display the date of the press release prominently.

☐ Put 'Press Release' at the top.

☐ Also write *For Immediate Publication* or *Embargoed to July xx* (if there is a reason for keeping the news until a later date) at the top.

☐ Use double-spacing or small paragraphs divided by a space.

☐ Keep it short: one page of between 400 and 500 words.

☐ Use one side of the paper only if you must go on to another page.

☐ Always finish with ENDS.

☐ Choose your font carefully. It must be easily readable and not quirky.

☐ Write with the journalist in mind. They are not looking to buy your product or service but to fill a news need.

☐ Write your press release asking yourself the question: 'Why should readers of *XYZ* care' rather than 'What's in it for me?'

☐ Start with an underlined heading encapsulating your reasons for sending this press release: (for example, Tom Glanville, award-winning chef from The Savoy to join The Dining Room, Bristol, as head chef).

☐ Develop the press release with newsworthy items, such as what strengths Tom will bring to the restaurant due to his culinary style and background. Tom may be hosting a sample menu tasting or he may be holding a charity promotion or offering cookery courses.

☐ Finally, add other details at the end (for example, Notes for editor: The Dining Room, owned and run by Jessica Yates, opened in 1999, is in the *Good Food Guide* and has two rosettes in the *AA Guide*. For further information and for photography contact Jessica Yates – with full contact details).

☐ Re-read your press release for grammatical errors and spelling mistakes.

☐ Send the press release by post. If sending via email, it may be ignored or deleted.

DEALING WITH CRITICS

Don't confuse advertorials with reviews. The former are part of the advertising process whereas the latter are unsolicited.

If you believe in your restaurant then you will welcome a critic, but only one who understands the restaurant business rather than a celebrity reviewer who may simply be out for themselves. Such reviewers are usually attention-seeking and have little respect within the restaurant industry. Restaurants generally deserve much better than the reviews these people give.

Critics can be vicious but can equally heap praise on where praise is due. I have been a restaurant critic and restaurant inspector for a number of years and, before that, I was a chef and restaurant owner. Not all critics have this background, of course, but it is immensely useful to have been steeped in the business before taking up the critical pen. Some restaurateurs grumble after a poor review that the critic was not an ordinary customer. There are, indeed, critics who set preposterous standards when reviewing a restaurant which has no pretensions. Such a person is not doing their job fairly or properly.

What critics look for

Criticism must be based on the food, the sourcing of the produce, the kitchen's skills, the front-of-house staff, the degree of care and attention shown to the customer and the degree of comfort (at least a decent chair to sit on rather than one that cuts into the backs of your legs).

It is not just the food the critic focuses on, however, but also the feel of the restaurant and if the experience was a successful, enjoyable one. Was hospitality offered? Creativity? Innovation? Maybe a theatrical buzz?

Criticism is worthless unless the writer can give reasons as to why the food, atmosphere or service was poor. It is simply not good enough to say, 'I didn't like my pork belly with pak choi.' Why not? Was it tough, too salty, the meat poorly sourced, the vegetable wildly overcooked? A critic owes it to the restaurant to explain why.

Critics do have the power to close a business. Their judgement can be that tough on businesses. I derive no pleasure from this. But some restaurateurs are simply not cut out to be in the business and do unutterable damage to the industry's reputation.

Responding to reviews

On the positive side, a good critique can create a boom time, the phone ringing non-stop for bookings. If this happens to you, give the critic a call or write to them. This is always appreciated.

> **TOP TIP**
> *how to books · small business · start-ups*
>
> What if you do receive a bad review? Ultimately, your customers are your best critics, but if there is a drop in the numbers coming through your door it may be time to reappraise your efforts. If a review was bad and you respect the writer for their style, understanding and fair points, then you must take it on board and resolve to address the criticism.

There will always be times in a restaurant's life when not everything runs smoothly: your chef burns a hand, a staff member hasn't removed the lipstick from a just-washed glass, a late produce delivery means too little time to prep properly. You will just have to accept the negative press reaction should a critic be in that evening. But it is simply no good relying on 'chef's night off' as an excuse. If the chef was off, the deputy should have achieved the same standards. Or you should have closed the restaurant that day/evening.

National critics respected by most restaurateurs and the public alike include Fay Maschler (*London Evening Standard*) and Jay Rayner (*Observer*). They know their onions and can deliver some pretty savage blows as well as praise when it's due. The ones not to take seriously include Michael Winner (*The Sunday Times*). Be very wary of approaching AA Gill (*The Sunday Times*) and Giles Coren (*The Times*). These can be harsh and they don't take prisoners.

Approaching critics

If you approach a restaurant critic with information about your restaurant in the hope you will receive a write-up, make sure you do so with your eyes wide open. It is a long shot that your restaurant will be chosen for a write-up by national papers, however. Many of these critics stay firmly in town, only venturing outside London occasionally during their 52 or fewer weeks of the year's reviewing.

However, regional newspapers that have such a column welcome reports of new restaurants opening or of changes of chef and, if they are worth their salt, they will do an anonymous write-up rather than accept an invitation to be your guest. I am always very pleased to know of changes in my home area of Hampshire and West Sussex and will put names on my list of restaurants to review. But I will never go as a guest because this it could be seen as compromising my objectivity.

THE GUIDES

Why aspire to have an entry in the guides? Depending on which guide you are in – preferably a non-fee-paying one – this will give you extra publicity and earn you respect. There are, however, good, mediocre and bad guides. Below I list the ones that matter in the trade, the ones restaurateurs aspire to achieve an entry in rather than the guides in which you pay to have an entry. Your customers are, generally speaking, a discerning lot and can sniff an advertising puff when they come across it.

Les Routiers is a case in point. Since its inception in 1935 in France, the famous blue-and-red symbol has indicated hotels and restaurants of individual character. These are often managed by the owner and offer 'good food, warm hospitality and excellent value for money.' And in the twenty-first century? These are still the guiding principles, according to Nicholas Stanley, Managing Director. Les Routiers Limited is a network of independent restaurants, pubs and hotels located in the UK and Ireland but also an 'umbrella organisation marking their shared values and individual appeal through the Les Routiers brand'. In short, you pay for the privilege and submit your own copy. Small restaurants are from £450, establishments with over 50 covers £600 for their marketing membership.

I wouldn't want anyone to spend a penny in some of the restaurants in the guide I have reviewed as a critic. Not only was the food bad but the service and establishment too. Paradoxically it also lists some very good restaurants, their management having taken the decision to spread their restaurant's publicity widely by having an entry in the guide. The choice, of course, is theirs and yours. If you wish to find out more about an entry, contact info@routiers.co.uk.

The top guides, as recognised by restaurateurs and customers, are without doubt *The Good Food Guide* and *The Michelin Guide* in the UK and Ireland. Other good guides include *The AA Restaurant Guide, Harden's UK Restaurants* (although not a favourite of many restaurateurs), *Time Out Eating and Drinking in Great Britain and Ireland, Time Out Eating and Drinking in London* and Georgina Campbell's *Jameson Guide Ireland. The Zagat Survey* can also be useful.

Submit your restaurant to guides with details of the menu, wine list and how to find you, together with a covering letter in the hope that an inspector may come calling.

The AA Restaurant Guide

This hefty tome lists 780 stand-alone restaurants and approximately 1,200 restaurants that are part of hotels. The AA has a mere 30 inspectors and awards AA rosettes. These go from one rosette for 'excellent local restaurants serving food prepared with care, understanding and skill, using good quality ingredients' to five rosettes, awarded to 'the finest restaurants in the British Isles, where cooking stands comparison with the best in the world'.

AA rosettes are awarded solely for the cooking and consistency, the standard to be achieved 'regardless of the chef's day off!' Ambience, style, comfort, the layout and presentation of the menu, appearance, the attitude and efficiency of service and the quality of the wine list 'should all fit the ambition of the cooking' too. There are other entries for non-rosette winners.

My quibble with the guide is its layout, with very busy pages and some inconsistencies, making it a bit of a challenge to negotiate and read. All that text, all those pictures, all those counties crashing into one another with hardly a gap. Are the inspectors discriminating enough? There are some entries I would not have put in but this is subjective. It is out of date too, with a number of restaurants that were closed way before the guide was printed. The maps are not easy on the eye either.

There is no payment for entry but pictures cost. The editor welcomes restaurants to submit their details for inspection and, hopefully, inclusion.

Website: www.theaa.com.

Georgina Campbell's Jameson Guide – Ireland's Best Places to Eat, Drink and Stay

Dubbed the 'glove-box bible', Georgina Campbell's is Ireland's most respected independently assessed hospitality guide. This meticulously researched guide features over 1,200 entries on where to eat, drink and stay in Ireland. From hotels, restaurants, cafes and pubs to country houses, guesthouses and farmhouses, this indefatigable writer, who conceived the guide in 1998, is particularly interested in highlighting restaurants keen on the provenance of their ingredients with the emphasis on quality. This guide has a rating system with a quirky demi-star denoting a restaurant approaching full-star status. Three stars is the highest rating.

There is a sister guide, Georgina Campbell's *Jameson Guide Dublin,* which lists restaurants by post code (as does the main guide in the capital) and by cuisine and speciality. Both assess entries independently and there is no payment for inclusion. No advertising is allowed by entries.

Website: www.ireland-guide.com.

The Good Food Guide

The Good Food Guide was first published in 1952. It was then taken up and published by the *Which? Consumers Guides* in 1962. It is the one found in keen diners' cars for searching for a recommended restaurant in town or country, with perhaps another copy at home for research or for simply drooling over the descriptions of food and places.

It is the voice of the consumer – the original ethos of the publication. It does not accept sponorship, advertising or free meals, and all the reviewers conduct their inspections anonymously.

Restaurants are not charged for inclusion in the guide. Contact the guide to let them know you exist, send in menus, a wine list and information about your restaurant and staff and hopefully an inspection will follow.

Website: www.which.net/goodfoodguide.

Harden's UK Restaurants

Harden's Guides, run by brothers Richard and Peter Harden, is a publishing firm based in London. Fifteen years ago, Richard and Peter launched their first and best-selling guide, *Harden's London Restaurants* – now the longest-established pocket guide to London restaurants. In 1998 a companion volume was launched: *Harden's UK Restaurants.*

The opinions expressed in both guides are based on what is now the largest annual survey of restaurant-goers in the UK (over 8,000 people took part for the 2006 edition, contributing over 90,000 reports). In addition the brothers say they have visited practically every restaurant listed in the London guide, and many of those listed in the UK volume. Their personal visits are always conducted anonymously, and at the firm's expense.

No fee is payable for inclusion in these guides nor is any advertising or hospitality accepted.

Website: www.hardens.com.

The Michelin Guide

The Michelin Guide, conceived in France in 1900 for hungry motorists, now has eight guides covering 21 European countries. The UK one was first published in 1974. It covers hotels and restaurants with minimal wording, its timeless symbols denoting facilities, features and categories.

The guide, published annually, employs only 70 full-time inspectors, who have training and experience in the hotel and catering industry for the whole of Europe. Each establishment 'is visited and/or tested by our staff at least once in the year', including many that don't make the grade.

The guide's restaurant ratings are probably the most recognized and influential culinary ratings in western Europe. The guide awards one to three stars to a small number of restaurants of outstanding quality. Stars are awarded sparingly.

This is the guide many chefs aspire to, a Michelin star adding huge kudos to the chef, the restaurant taking second place. If the chef decamps, the star is lost to both the chef and restaurant.

Three Michelin stars: 'Exceptional cuisine, worth a special journey – one always eats here extremely well, sometimes superbly. Fine wines, faultless service, elegant surroundings. One will pay accordingly.'

Two Michelin stars: 'Excellent cooking, worth a detour – specialities and wines of first class quality. This will be reflected in the price.'

One Michelin star: 'A very good restaurant in its category – the star indicates a good place to stop on your journey. But beware of comparing the star given to an expensive "de luxe" establishment to that of a simple restaurant where you can appreciate fine cooking at a reasonable price.'

Other restaurant symbols include crossed knives and forks – one to five – which denote the degree of comfort, the latest addition being a fork and mug for traditional pubs serving good food.

The Bib Gourmand, with the Michelin man's head in red, denotes good food at moderate prices at a less elaborate restaurant.

Michelin updates

In the past it was considered that, in order to gain a star, lavish comfort was an irrefutable necessity. This has been relaxed considerably due to changing, more informal times.

A former Michelin inspector wrote a controversial book about the guide, stating that the gourmet restaurant bible was understaffed, out of date and in thrall to big-name chefs in France. A number of restaurateurs and critics were not taken aback by these criticisms because they felt the guide had lost some of its authority. Despite this, it is still seen by many as a true reflection of good restaurants (and hotels) in the 21 countries featured in the eight published guides. Inclusion is free. The *UK Guide* is published in mid-January.

Website: www.themichelinguide-gbirl@uk.michelin.com.

Time Out Eating and Drinking in Great Britain and Ireland *and* The Time Out London Eating and Drinking Guide

The London guide, first published in 1983, was followed by the Great Britain and Ireland one in 2004, with 1,200 entries in each well produced, independent publication. These are the guides that are the most helpful and readable and they come from the large *Time Out* stable of guides.

London guide

In the London guide, restaurants are considerately grouped into types and ethnicity (brasserie, pubs, wine bars, Greek, Italian, Thai, for example), eating on a budget and by area. There is also a useful list of where to do brunch, Sunday lunch, late eating, eating alone, taking a date, taking the kids, spotting a celeb, finding the unfamiliar and loving the look.

It includes a list of new restaurants and closures, and immensely good boxed information giving the lowdown on Sri Lankan, Thai, Indian food, etc., with explanations of words and dishes you may find on menus.

A red star denotes a very good restaurant of its type, a green star a more budget-conscious eatery. Annual awards are given for best bar, pub, local restaurant, gastro pub, family restaurant, Indian restaurant, cheap eat, vegetarian meal, design, new restaurant and outstanding achievement.

Great Britain and Ireland guide

This is a small volume in comparison, but is a very welcome addition, uses the same star system and other helpful information. The regional listing includes London, but I do question why some of the entries in both volumes have been included and others left out.

The writers are around 50 'mostly' freelance inspectors (mainly food journalists). These are good, clear maps in both guides. There is no payment to be included in either book. 'Places are re-reviewed each year.'

Website: www.timeout.com.

The Zagat Survey

Started by New Yorkers Tim and Nina Zagat in 1979, there has been a *London Restaurant Guide* for years. This is just one of the many guides in the US and Europe to have emerged via a survey which invites diners to rate and review restaurants and many other leisure pursuits they have visited.

However, this quirky read can become tiresome, even though it does have a location index, useful 'all-day dining', 'breakfast/brunch' and many more categories to look up. It is not always up to date and not widely known, except for aficionados of the genre.

Website: www.zagat.com.

Local lists

Your local tourist information office may have a list of restaurants to which you can add your business. Scout around the web to link your restaurant to your area – there may be other websites you can be part of.

Contact the local media via a press release if your restaurant is entered in a prestigious guide. Contact the national media if you have been awarded a Michelin star, an AA rosette or are given a high rating in *The Good Food Guide*.

EXPANDING YOUR BUSINESS

There are slack times in the restaurant trade. Think therefore of adding some extra strings to your bow, such as cookery classes, outside catering, takeaway, writing for a local or national magazine or newspaper, or targeting the corporate market with special lunch deals.

Loyalty cards and comment cards

If you are running a fast, casual restaurant, consider a loyalty or privilege card that many corporate coffee businesses, such as Caffe Nero, offer. The card accumulates points against future purchases, with *x* number of points for a free coffee, *xxx* points for a meal for two.

Comment cards are good for market research purposes, the card's tick boxes including the customer's name and address and/or email address, cleanliness, service, food enjoyment, welcome, etc., with a few lines for customers' comments.

Cookery classes

If you are a good communicator, why not capitalise on your premises and your skills to create a series of cookery classes and/or demonstrations? These can be instead of the lunch trade one day (choose a slack day) every month or when your restaurant has a weekly closing day.

Write to your customers via a newsletter, put up posters and distribute flyers in the restaurant, in libraries, shops and elsewhere in your area. Outline a daily, weekly or monthly set of classes for six or more paying students (it generally won't pay to have fewer), depending on your kitchen size.

Design the classes carefully around your own prep time, leaving plenty of time to clear up, to have some time off and to prepare for the evening.

 Plan the cooking with a domestic kitchen in mind and don't use hard-to-find ingredients. Don't be too technically advanced or you may lose your students. Have a member of staff in to wash up during the class, and help prep before the students arrive. Put this cost into your budget.

Possible timetable 1: 9.30 am arrive: coffee and talk. 10 am: start students cooking a two-course meal (or whatever you have chosen to do). 12.30: lunch with a glass of wine in restaurant. 2 pm: discussion of cooking and questions and answers. Departure: 3.30 pm with pack containing recipes, restaurant menus, public relations information.

Possible timetable 2: 10 am: arrival and coffee. Demonstration: 11 am–12.30 pm. Glass of wine with food either still in the kitchen or informally in the restaurant. Leave 1.30 with tips and recipe pack plus menu and public relations informations.

Offer gift vouchers for classes and demonstrations.

Types of classes
You could teach the following:

☐ The basics: soups, breads, patés, roasts, simple desserts, jams, biscuits.

☐ Cooking for family and friends: simple oven dishes using chicken or pasta.

☐ Food from Morocco, Spain, Italy, France, Thailand, Mexico, each country covered by a series of hands-on cooking classes or demonstrations.

☐ Cooking with spices and chillies.

☐ Cooking with fish (e.g. learning how to skin and fillet fish), meat, game, shellfish, vegetables.

☐ Pasta (learning how to make pasta and sauces).

☐ Men in the kitchen day.

☐ Cooking for children and with children from scratch.

☐ Entertaining at home.

☐ Vegetarian food.

☐ Tapas.

☐ Simple starters.

☐ Party desserts.

☐ Party buffets.

☐ Party canapés.

☐ How to get through Christmas as the family cook.

You could also organise a demo masterclass by your restaurant's chef(s) or ask a local celebrity chef/food writer to do a demonstration.

The most popular cookery courses are Christmas, men, children and entertaining, but other subjects can easily grab the imagination if presented well and clearly on paper. Calculate your costs carefully before deciding on a price per person. Offer discounts for group bookings: one comes free if they books six friends, for example. Make sure your classes measure up to expectations (i.e. don't promise more than you can fulfil). Ask your students to fill in a questionnaire before departure for feedback. You may be surprised how much good market research you can obtain.

Outside catering

Your kitchen is an obvious place to capitalise on your assets as well as your skills and those of your staff. Outside catering may be a way forward during quiet times. Or you may be able to offer your restaurant customers and others a full year-round outside catering service if you have enough space, equipment and staff.

☐ Work out carefully what your staff and space can handle.

☐ Plan your outside catering menus around these constraints.

☐ You might be able to offer hot and cold food; a canapé and buffet service; three-course sit-down meals; full wedding parties; a hamper service for sporting or musical events; extra chefs and waiting staff.

☐ Consider whether you will hire or buy in equipment, if you have separate space for the storage of food and drink for outside catering and refrigeration and hygiene matters.

☐ Will you be able to give a fair share of your time to discuss outside catering clients' needs? This can be time-consuming, with visits to the client's house or to where the party is to be held.

☐ Make a supply list and a work schedule, and plan transportation and staffing.

☐ Communication with the client is everything. Failure to do this may jeopardise the party and your reputation.

☐ The day after the party can also mean clearing up and sorting out equipment.

☐ Don't jeopardise your restaurant by taking on too much too soon.

☐ If you decide to do outside catering or a takeaway service, have printed catering menus for customers to pick up.

☐ Open accounts with companies for breakfasts, lunches, special events or a takeaway trade. Make provisos, such as payment terms of 30 days and trade references, and stipulate a minimum order and a 24-hour cancellation notice.

But first the essentials

Marketing, selling, planning and organisation are essential tools.

☐ Do your homework first. What do local catering companies offer?

☐ Identify your market and communicate with them by letter, flyers, etc.

☐ Create business cards and general menus to go on to flyers.

☐ Don't give out prices over the phone but offer the caller a tailor-made menu to be sent in writing after initial discussion of the event, with several price and menu alternatives.

☐ Have all the arrangements in writing and agreed on both sides.

☐ Ask for a deposit. Some outside caterers ask for one third when booking, one third two weeks in advance and the balance on the day of the event. Others ask for 10 per cent when the booking takes place, then half minus the 10 per cent, then the balance on the day. If you are dealing with corporate clients, you may decide on invoicing them after the event, following an initial deposit.

☐ Inform your client of a deposit forfeit should the party be cancelled.

☐ Inform your client of cancellation charges closer to the event.

☐ Also inform them of your need to know the final numbers one week before the party.

☐ Keep any letters of recommendation and testimonials to show to prospective clients.

☐ Take photographs of food, events and staff for your records and for marketing.

☐ Keep the dialogue going by contacting customers whom you have sent information to. Don't expect to win them all, though!

Corporate lunches

Service, service, service can often supersede location, location, location thanks to a fast turnaround at lunchtime. Business lunches should be snappy and well managed. It is, therefore, worth considering attracting this market if your restaurant is close to a number of large or medium-sized businesses.

Draw up a list of businesses in your area. Contact the administration or human resources department and find out a name to write to. Prepare a welcoming letter outlining what you can offer the company at lunchtime or for other corporate entertaining, either at your restaurant or as outside catering at the business.

Discuss with your chef the type of dishes that can be offered with swiftness and good value in mind. Prepare some sample menus and send these with the welcoming letter to the member of staff you have located, adding business cards and copies of good reviews or testimonials from other companies. Cold starters and desserts are obvious choices that can be plated quickly. Simply cooked main courses, such as grilled fish, meat and pasta, are ideal. A plate of the best charcuterie with pickles and salads is also popular.

 **A glass of wine or soft drink and coffee are added incentives within the price per person, but beware. If you offer poor-quality wine or coffee to keep costs down, repeat business may not come your way.**

Some restaurants, such as Bistro Montparnasse in Portsmouth, offer a lunch that gives little by way of profit. This lunch showcases what the restaurant can offer. Business people will return in the evening with friends and family for a more relaxed meal, having been assured of good food and service. This is excellent marketing.

You may be able to offer a food-delivery service to companies' boardrooms. Supply such food as croissants filled with ham and cheese, cream cheese and crispy bacon, tortilla wraps with a mix of fish, meat and vegetarian fillings, salad bowls, specialist bread sandwiches, bite-size fruit bowls and drinks.

Set up corporate credit accounts, and stipulate a minimum order with 24-hours' notice and a 24-hour cancellation notice to safeguard your business and your blood pressure!

Writing a column or a cookbook

These are two excellent ways of keeping your restaurant's profile in the media. But you must consider your skills and your time. Can you write clearly, concisely and interestingly? Will your column's recipes be user-friendly for the general public? Think whether you can fit in the writing as well as cooking and/or running a restaurant, and whether you have something offbeat or unusual to impart in a cookbook.

If you believe you have these attributes, here are some steps you could take:

☐ Contact your local paper, magazine or radio station and talk to the features editor or programme producer about a column, or find out their name and write to them outlining what you have in mind.

☐ Write a one-page letter, explaining your column in clear, concise language. Include your culinary attributes and other background which may be of interest – but only if relevant.

☐ Go to a bookstore and look at the cookbooks on offer. Which books would you like to emulate and why? Obtain their publishers' names.

☐ Highlight a good story you have to tell about your restaurant: how you grow your own vegetables, herbs and salads, raise chickens for the pot, all in the back of beyond. Describe your expertise with unusual puddings or terrines, your exotic culinary pzazz, or that yours has been a family-run restaurant for generations.

☐ Contact the commissioning editors by name either in writing or by phone.

☐ Invest in *The Writer's Handbook* (Macmillan www.panmacmillan.com) for UK publishers, agents, national and regional newspapers and other useful information, or *The Guardian Media Guide* (Atlantic Books) for similar guidance and other media information. Both available at large bookstores.

☐ Contact the Guild of Food Writers (www.gfw.co.uk) for advice.

It takes time and perseverance to get on this particular ladder, as I can testify to, but dogged determination can pay off.

Don't:

☐ write complex recipes to which only chefs can aspire;

☐ write a book unless you have a distinctive, different 'voice'; or

☐ take on too much media work – writing a column, a book, TV, radio – because this may take you away from those stoves for too long, and your business will suffer as a result.

 Take a good break from time to time to restore your brain power and to gain inspiration.

8

STAFFING THE WELL RUN RESTAURANT

Good restaurants create quality, consistent, well sourced food in a pleasing atmosphere with service to match. In order to achieve this, chefs and front-of-house staff should be equally creative, consistent, welcoming and professional. And calm.

Temperamental chefs do exist – and not only on television – but these people are best avoided as no one can operate in such an atmosphere and do their best cooking or other kitchen work. Their attitude rubs off on other staff, so choose your chefs – and other staff – prudently. Front-of-house managers can be equally domineering. Intimidating verbal behaviour and, especially, physical abuse, should not to be tolerated in your kitchen or restaurant.

 TOP TIP — *how to books • small business start-ups*

As most restaurateurs will testify, staff are the biggest problem *and* the biggest asset a restaurant can have.

This chapter deals with:

- ☐ staffing problems;
- ☐ college and agency recruitment;
- ☐ catering management;
- ☐ interviewing and job descriptions;
- ☐ kitchen hierarchy;
- ☐ job commitment;
- ☐ staff organisation and training;
- ☐ pay legalities;

☐ job analysis and empowering staff; and

☐ basic waiting and management skills, table reservations, and duty and cleaning rotas.

It also covers dress code, staff meals, holidays, smoking, behaviour and how to communicate effectively with customers.

THE IMPORTANCE OF SERVICE

Service, service, service is fast overtaking location, location, location in today's competitive restaurant marketplace. As standards rise in the quality of the produce and comfort, so must the service which, of course, covers all kitchen, waiting and cleaning staff and any other employees in a restaurant.

Personal service and attention to detail set the best restaurants apart. This applies to the smallest café, the out-of-the-way gastro pub, a town-centre or neighbourhood restaurant or a wine bar.

The right mix

There is no doubt that restaurant work is demanding: some see it as drudgery while others see it as a challenge that is both stimulating and rewarding.

Restaurants are sometimes described as like a theatre and, while many exponents of this profession love to entertain, they should always remember their serious professional stance and couple this with humour, good judgement and sensitivity.

Staff need direction, motivation and incentive to carry out their work and should understand the need to be very flexible. This all comes from the management.

Front-of-house staff

The front-of-house staff should be acceptable to both sexes, have the ability to make their customers feel at ease and be trusted for their judgement.

Waiting staff

Waiters – skilled ones – offer service. They know their menu and are aware of their power to make a meal one to remember or one to forget. They are not servants. They have talked to the kitchen about the composition of the food and are able to advise which combinations go best together if the customer isn't sure what to choose. Two cream dishes in succession are to be avoided, for example.

They are aware when to clear a table and when not to. When to pour wine. When a customer is becoming restless for the bill. They are also aware of tips and how to generate this extra income. Anyone can wait on tables, but just how natural are they, and are they an asset to your business or not?

Kitchen staff

Kitchen staff are creative in different ways. Chefs have the ability to prepare food, timing cooking to a split second with speed and accuracy. They can cook and present all the dishes coming out of the kitchen. They must be able to do this time and time again to the same high standard. Consistency is all.

FINDING STAFF

Catering colleges are one source of kitchen staff, but the standards of some are decidedly questionable. The teaching focuses on a hotel-like service which is past its sell-by date, according to employers. Flour-based sauces, soups and stocks made from packets, and heavy, stodgy food are compounded by outmoded silver service (useful perhaps for banqueting) and folding napkins into unnecessary shapes, amongst other contentious catering issues.

Some colleges have moved on and are teaching their students the art of lighter cooking combined with slow-food cooking (daubes, terrines, bread-making). They are sourcing their materials with care and attention and teaching how to run a kitchen, amongst other modern and commercial necessities. These are the chefs who will be able to deliver the consistently high standards customers expect and good restaurateurs wish to achieve.

However, when leaving college some students, feel they have wasted their time. The real world is different and so they have to start the whole learning process all over again.

Restaurant employers are also handicapped by some students' and non-trained staff's backgrounds. The type of food they experience at home can be at variance with the food offered in restaurants, which they may have no interest in. There may be a mountain to climb in food education but, when a staff member sees the light and becomes excited about the type and quality of the food and service, this is a wonderful moment.

Some of those who enter the profession also see the catering trade as a way to become famous – to follow in the shoes of the Jamie Olivers of this world but without having to work too hard. Unlike Jamie, who started at the bottom and proved himself.

If during an interview a prospective member of staff asks how much they will be paid and how much time off they will get, without asking pertinent questions about the restaurant and the job, then it's hardly worth continuing with the interview.

Sources of recruitment

A small restaurant needs a good chef who is able to communicate and teach their perhaps younger staff. They need to be able to instil in their staff a passion about sourcing excellent produce and cooking it with skill and care. Apprenticeship is alive and well and should be encouraged vigorously, with many students attending day-release courses while they are working in a restaurant kitchen.

Train local people. Create a good team by encouraging their creative side, but with good, solid guidelines laid down either by management or by a head chef. Kitchens that work well are staffed by local people who enjoy being together and creating good food and service.

Your staff must be able to cover for one another in times of crisis or staff absence, making sure that the whole service runs as smoothly and pleasantly as possible. Whingers, clock watchers and lazy people can infect a good team.

Recruitment agencies

Catering agencies are employment agencies but dedicated to this specific industry. They may place staff permanently or temporarily. An agency charges at least 10 per cent of the agreed wage, and the agency staff then work for a probationary period. On completion of this period, the agency invoices the company for their percentage.

It is important to weigh up the costs and advantages of recruiting agency staff. On the plus side, many agencies get to know their applicants well and match appropriate chefs to appropriate businesses. It's not in their interests to get this wrong but, of course, this can and does happen because some agencies see a chef as merely making money for them. Agencies aren't cheap, and you may achieve just as good (if not better) results with an ad that may attract a greater number of applicants.

Temporary agency staff are usually better paid per hour. This may cause friction once your other staff know their hourly rate doesn't match the temp's pay, so try not to create this mix if possible.

Promote from within. It is easier and more cost effective to find a commis chef from an agency than to go to an agency to recruit a higher-up position.

The chef may be able to train up a commis chef who has been with the company for a while to the higher grade.

Other sources of staff include:

☐ advertising;

☐ job centres;

☐ headhunters;

☐ existing staff;

☐ a waiting list – people coming to the restaurant looking for a job;

☐ previous applicants;

☐ casual callers; and

☐ the education system.

MOTIVATING YOUR STAFF

If you look at the restaurant industry, with its uniforms, differing job titles, tipping, unsocial hours, labour mobility, irregular work flow and entrepreneurship, you will see that the catering industry is certainly unique. Because it is unique, one thing is for sure: you must be organised. This means good staffing at all levels, staff who are flexible, who understand speed when busy but who do not forgo quality. They must have the ability to do other jobs, such as cleaning, and must undergo extra training if necessary during less busy times. Motivation by management is paramount to keeping good staff. Job satisfaction cannot be underestimated.

Unskilled staff

The reasons why unskilled catering work is popular are:

☐ the work is easy to learn;

☐ there is variety;

☐ it is not a factory;

☐ you meet people; and

☐ its an easy way to earn quick money and doesn't have to be permanent.

How to motivate people

To hold on to your staff, you should employ good management practices:

☐ Communicating clearly.

☐ Not over-controlling.

☐ Recognising achievement. This will result in increased performance.

☐ Good teaching.

☐ Rewarding adequately.

☐ Reviewing performance on a regular basis.

☐ Treating your staff like human beings and not like cogs in a machine.

☐ Making promises and then not delivering them.

☐ Taking what people say seriously. Listening to your staff.

☐ Investigating complaints or grievances.

☐ Avoiding deals.

☐ Making your staff realise they are a real team.

☐ Recognising a career commitment.

People may become attached to a team because they have something in common rather than working for the same business (e.g. they are all students, all women, all the same age). If this is the case, work on these shared characteristics and build up their bond.

GETTING OFF TO A GOOD START

Although a job description can set out all the usual conditions involved in a job, such as the work entailed, the hours of work, shift times, payment, staff meals, behaviour and dress, it can't describe what effort will be required to do the job properly. It is, therefore, a good idea to take on an applicant for a trial period before offering them a permanent job.

If you are taking on new chefs, ask them to cook a dish or two from your menu then sit down with them and, over the tasting, discuss with them the outcome and what they would be able to contribute to the menu and style of cooking. Although this may seem a lengthy process, at least you will be able to choose a good chef rather than one who may look good on paper but can't cook the simplest of dishes. And it will save you time and money in the long run.

During this process, you will be able to find out if the chef is familiar with and knows how to cook the ingredients on your menu. If the chef is unable to rise to the challenge of cooking steamed sea bass with a fennel sauce, for example, or even the best omelette, then you may not be talking the same culinary language.

To circumvent this procedure and to save time and money, find out as much as possible over the phone or by other means of communication before agreeing to an interview – and the cook-off.

Culinary checklist

You may also wish to have a culinary checklist asking, for example: 'What is your strongest area? Is there any section of the kitchen you feel less secure in?'

Some possible subjects for the checklist include the following:

Which can you cook?/did you cook in your last job?

☐ patés and terrines;

☐ soups;

☐ breads;

☐ canapés;

☐ ice creams;

☐ sauces;

☐ dressings;

☐ game;

☐ fish;

☐ egg dishes: omelettes, eggs Benedict?

Have you had any experience of the following?

☐ butchery;

☐ larder;

☐ working out the kitchen's gross profits;

☐ menu costing;

☐ purchasing?

Don't underestimate the person who applies for a job without qualifications and experience. If this person displays real enthusiasm and knowledge of food and has a passion for cooking and learning, they may be just the one to take on for a trial period. They may have that creative side that those with certificates lack.

The objectives of the employment interview

The employment interview should be used to:

☐ decide if the applicant is suitable for the job or, conversely, how suitable the job is for the applicant;

☐ decide if the applicant will fit into the existing team and into the organisation;

☐ get across the essential expectations and requirements of the job. The interview can be seen as part of the induction process;

☐ gather information, evaluate it and make a judgement;

☐ find out about the applicant's skills, experience and character; and

☐ assess the applicant's interest in the business.

Ask open questions, not ones that can only yield a 'yes' or 'no' answer:

☐ Tell me about your present job.

☐ What do you enjoy most about your job?

☐ Can you give me some examples?

☐ What did you enjoy about college?

☐ What did you get out of it?

☐ What made you decide to apply for the job?

☐ How do you find dealing with staff?

☐ Have you ever dealt with an unco-operative employee and what was the outcome?

☐ How do you feel about moving to this part of the country?

☐ How will this affect your home life?

When interviewing staff either for kitchen or front of house, ask for references and *follow them up*.

During the interview

Get across to potential staff the kind of high standards you expect from them, including dress, cleanliness (are those nails and shoes clean?), behaviour (fag breaks are few and far between, for example, and not within eyesight of customers), their flexibility (can they be called upon to do shifts at short notice?), their attitude to customers and the necessity of teamwork.

Find out if they are familiar with the type of food on offer and are willing to learn. Do they understand about wine and drinks service? If not, are they keen to find out? Can they work under pressure? With a smile? Are they motivated? Do they like working as part of a team? Do they look at you in the eye?

You may sense that they are only working for the money and will be out the door when the shift ends, not willing to add to the harmony and efficiency of the restaurant if extra tidying up, or paperwork, for example, are necessary.

Do you, in turn, give the impression of good management and organisation? Do you offer a decent wage according to experience and skills? Do you come across as a caring person whom staff can come to in times of need? Are you approachable? Do you give enough information about your staff needs and expectations? Or will you spring something on them that wasn't mentioned in interview after they have started working for you? You should offer a clear, concise contract, with hours, duties and pay structure.

If an employee is to respond to a customer's needs, they must know what the product or service is, its full breadth and its limits; what the business can do and cannot do because false promises to customers – and staff – can end in tears and recrimination. They also need to know the rules of the organisation and how to be sensitive and discreet.

This knowledge must be given to the employee and is not found out by chance. Careful role definition and training are a necessity.

OTHER EMPLOYMENT TIPS

Drawing up a job description

No matter how simple or low-level the job, the more information you include in the job description the better your chances of recruiting the right person. Include such things as skills needed, any necessary training and how much experience and responsibility the job requires.

References

Always take up the references; For a fuller, more in-depth account of the applicant, phone the referee and ask questions such as 'would you re-employ this person?'

Making your employees feel welcome

First impressions count, and the first three months of employment with a new boss and new colleagues are very important. Make your new employee feel welcome. Don't just pass them by and say 'are you all right?' Spend a few minutes with them to find out if they are feeling included and whether the job is not giving them difficulties but pleasure and satisfaction – or the reverse. Give praise where praise is due. Keep a list of their birthdays and either wish them 'happy birthday' or give them a card (if your business isn't too large to make this act of kindness).

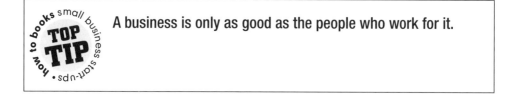

A business is only as good as the people who work for it.

Involve your employees in your work culture from day one and keep them up to date with the progress of the restaurant, especially any plans for future developments. Finding out about such things from a third party could lead to feels of disenchantment.

Appraising your staff regularly

Set up a review system for each staff member. Your business may have changed, perhaps creating more work. They may be finding this extra work difficult to accommodate without a dip in quality and service. Discuss important issues with the full team.

Enforcing strict 'absence' procedures

To deal effectively with absenteeism and late arrival at work, your staff should be very clear about your company's policy. A staff handbook is an ideal way to state your policies clearly, even if this is stored on an in-house computer rather than printed.

Outline clearly such things as holidays, sickness, absenteeism, lateness, dress code, make-up, jewellery, hair colour, type of shoes, your smoking policy and using mobile phones at work. This applies to restaurants of all sizes.

Overtime

A couple of phone calls are sometimes all you need to arrange overtime. Simple. Overtime, however, can undermine the quality of service and it can also undermine recruitment. People like to earn more money but this can result in tiredness. As a result, your staff will simply go through the motions and take short cuts.

The longer a vacancy exists, the more your staff become used to earning extra money. When a new member of staff does join the team, they may cause resentment because your other staff's wages will decrease.

EMPLOYING PEOPLE

When you employ people, the first thing to do is to call the New Employers' Helpline on (0845) 60 70 143. An adviser will set up an employment record and will send you an employer's starter pack. This pack includes all the information you need, such as a help book on paying someone for the first time, a working sheet to record your employees' pay and a employee's payment record. You could also ask for help with your payroll from your local Business Support Team. All these services are free and you can also attend a local workshop on payrolls (go to www.inlandrevenue.gov.uk/bst/index.htm).

As an employer you will be responsible for the following:

☐ Working out the tax and National Insurance contributions due each pay day.

☐ Keeping accurate and up-to-date records to back up any deduction in your accounts for wages, payments, benefits and such like relating to your employees.

☐ Making payments of statutory sick and maternity pay to your employees as appropriate.

☐ Making student loan deductions from an employee's earnings when directed by the Inland Revenue.

☐ Paying tax credits to employees when directed by the Inland Revenue.

☐ Paying deductions made over to the Inland Revenue Accounts Office each month – or quarterly if your average monthly payments are below £1,500 – after offsetting any tax credit payments.

☐ At the end of the tax year (April 5), telling the Inland Revenue how much each of your employees has earned and how much tax and NIC (National Insurance contributions) deductions you have made. You must also give details of any expenses paid or benefits provided to your employees.

Useful telephone numbers and websites:

Help with PAYE (Pay As You Earn) and/or NIC (National Insurance contributions) for new employers: (0845) 60 70 143.

National minimum wage helpline: (0845) 600 0678.

Employers' orderline for forms and stationery orders: (08457) 646 646.

Useful leaflets and pamphlets via www.inlandrevenue.gov.uk

The law on pay and hours of work

Legislation is based on British labour law and European social policy for working hours and minimum pay levels, the focus being on:

☐ limiting working hours;

☐ protection from pressure to work excessive hours;

☐ guaranteed holiday pay;

☐ guaranteed rest periods; and

☐ guaranteed minimum pay.

National minimum wage

There are three levels of minimum wage. The rates from 1 October 2008 are:

☐ £5.73 per hour for workers aged 22 years and older;

☐ development rate of £4.77 per hour for workers aged 18–21 inclusive; and

☐ £3.53 per hour for all workers under the age of 18 who are no longer of compulsory school age.

Development rate

The development rate for workers aged 22 and over was abolished for pay reference periods starting on or after 1 October 2006. All workers aged 22 and over who qualify for the national minimum wage are now entitled to the main rate of national minimum wage. This applies even where the worker was previously in receipt of the development rate for those aged 22 and over and had been receiving that rate for less than six months.

Compulsory school age

In England and Wales, a person is no longer of compulsory school age after the last Friday of June of the school year in which their sixteenth birthday occurs. In Scotland, pupils whose sixteenth birthday falls between 1 March and 30 September may not leave before 31 May of that year. Pupils aged 16 on or between 1 October and the last day of February may not leave until the start of the Christmas holidays in that school year. In Northern Ireland, a person is no longer of compulsory school age after 30 June of the school year in which their sixteenth birthday occurs.

Accommodation offset

The daily rate of the accommodation offset is £4.46 (£31.22 per week) for each day that accommodation is provided.

Working time and pay regulations

An employer must not require workers or employees to work more than an average of 48 hours a week, though workers and employees may choose to work longer.

☐ An employer must limit the normal working hours of night workers to an average of eight hours in any 24-hour period. Although this doesn't affect restaurants as such, there may be some restaurants in the future that open 24 hours.

☐ An entitlement to daily, weekly and in-work rest and four weeks' paid annual leave.

☐ Under the Employment Rights Act 2002 an employer must provide all employees with an individual written pay statement at or before the time of payment. This must show gross pay and take-home pay with amounts and reasons for variable and fixed deductions. Or fixed deductions can be shown as a total sum, provided a written statement of these items is given in advance to each employee at least once a year.

☐ An employer must not make unauthorised deductions from wages, including complete non-payment.

Part-time workers' regulations

These are very applicable to the restaurant business where many staff members are part-timers. Unfortunately, the regulations are poorly adhered, to but part-time employees must not be treated less favourably than full-time employees, and their contractual terms and conditions should be equal in terms of pay, pensions, annual holidays and training.

For further information go to: www.dti.gov.uk/er/ptime.htm.

Employing foreign nationals

Nationals from Austria, Belgium, Cyprus, Italy, Liechtenstein, Denmark, Finland, France, Germany, Greece, Iceland, Ireland, Malta, the Netherlands, Norway, Spain and Sweden can work freely in the UK. Nationals from Cyprus and Malta have full free movement rights and are not required to obtain a workers registration certificate.

European Economic Area (EEA) and Swiss nationals and members of their family who are living in the UK can apply for a registration certificate or a residence card to confirm the holder's rights of residence under European law. EEA and Swiss nationals and their families can apply for confirmation of permanent residence after living in the UK for five years.

Nationals of the Czech Republic, Estonia, Hungary, Latvia, Lithuania, Poland, Slovakia or Slovenia must register with the worker registration scheme when they take work in the UK. Bulgarian and Romanian nationals can apply for permission to work in the UK. Bulgarian and Romanian nationals cannot start work in the UK without permission.

For details go to: www.ukba.homeoffice.gov.uk.

Many Australians, New Zealanders, Canadians and other Commonwealth nationals also come to Britain to work, with a good number of them working in the restaurant trade. Under the Working Holidaymakers Scheme, 17–30-year-olds may work in Britain for two years. They may work full or part-time and can apply once only and must have the stamp or endorsement clearly marked on their passport for the employer to check.

For a full list of Commonwealth members and for other information regarding employing foreign nationals, obtain *Comprehensive Guidance for United Kingdom Employers on Changes in the Law on Preventing Illegal Working* from www.ind.homeoffice.gov.uk. Or call the employers' helpline (0845) 010 6677 for a booklet.

To obtain a National Insurance number, a foreign national attends an 'evidence of identity' interview at their nearest job centre, taking with them their passport or proof of identity as well as evidence they are working. For further details, go to: www.workingintheuk.gov.uk.

Maternity rights

The legislation concerning pregnant employees includes the following:

☐ Employers are required to protect the health and safety of employees who are pregnant, have recently given birth or are breast-feeding.

☐ These protections start as soon as the employee is pregnant.

☐ The contract of employment throughout the 18 weeks' ordinary maternity leave or any additional leave must be continued unless either party to the contract ends it or it expires.

☐ During maternity leave the employee should continue to receive all her contractual benefits except wages.

☐ An employer must not dismiss an employee or select her for redundancy in preference to other comparable employees during her pregnancy or maternity leave just because she is pregnant.

For further information go to: www.dti.gov.uk/er/maternity.htm.

Redundancy payment

If you dismiss an employee by reason of redundancy, you are required to make a lump sum payment to that employee based on their age, length of service and rate of pay at the time of their dismissal.

For further information contact (0870) 1502 500 or go to the Department of Trade and Industry's website (www.dti.gov.uk/regs).

Unfair dismissal

An employee who believes they have been unfairly dismissed can complain to an employment tribunal, generally subject to a qualifying period of one year's continuous service. Complaints can be made regardless of the length of service if the dismissal is for certain specified reasons (e.g. pregnancy or maternity leave).

Trade union membership

All employees have a right to belong, or not to belong, to a trade union. It is unlawful to refuse a person employment because they either are or are not a member of a trade union. It is also unlawful for employees to be dismissed or discriminated against because of their membership or non-membership of a trade union.

Staff meals

One of the worst things you can do is to palm your staff off with a poor meal while they are on duty. What it says is that you don't value them. How will they learn about the food they are preparing and serving if they aren't offered it? They will have much more respect for you if given a meal that is nourishing, delicious and shared by all at table before service.

Jill Dupleix, former *The Times'* cook and author, passed by London's Kensington Place restaurant and spied staff sitting down to huge bowls of penne with meatballs and a green salad. Another meal at Zilli Fish in Covent Garden was equally admired by Jill as staff ate a roasting tray of fat sardines sizzling in garlic and tomatoes, spaghetti with a chilli sauce, and roasted red peppers and chicken thighs with a pizzaiola-style sauce.

In other words, this doesn't have to cost the earth. A good meal helps to create a happy team. And if your waiting staff eat some of the dishes on the menu they will be better prepared to sell it.

 Happy bosses and happy staff make happy customers.

KITCHEN HIERARCHY TERMINOLOGY

The professional kitchen's cooking staff are known as the *brigade*. Like many kitchen words, this comes from the French and, further back, from *brigata*, an Italian word for a company or crew, so its origins are military. Look up the word in an Italian dictionary and ironically you'll find it comes from the verb *brigare*, 'to brawl, wrangle or fight'.

The ideal restaurant staff

The size of the brigade is dependent on the establishment. Many small restaurants are based on a head chef, a sous chef and/or a commis chef plus, hopefully, a kitchen porter whose job is mainly to wash up. Or your staff may simply be the chef, who relies on the waiting staff to help out with washing up and lesser preparations, such as plating desserts and prepping breads, butter and ancillaries.

Large restaurants will have an executive chef, a head chef, senior and junior sous ('under', from the French), chefs, chefs de partie (those responsible for a section of the kitchen, e.g. sauces, larder, starters, mains, vegetables and desserts), demi-chefs de partie (literally 'half') and a commis (first and second) chef. A commis – a deputy or clerk – learns their trade from the bottom of the hierarchy. They are there to help, learn and watch. There may also be a (rare) chef tournant, an all-purpose chef who is capable of all sections and who may be filling in for absent/holidaying chefs.

The following are definitions from the lowest to the highest rank.

Kitchen porter (KP)
Respect your KP, as they are affectionately known. Their job is the unenviable one of washing pots, utensils, glasses, plates – the lot – and they may also be offered the joys of prepping vegetables and washing salads. Be kind to your KP because they must endure the repetitive tasks that are the underpinnings of the system.

The commis chef
This is not the dream job envisaged by some but this is the job to learn by. Duties may include plating up garnishes for all courses, with some cooking, including stocks. Depending on the size of the restaurant, they may also deal with stock-taking and deliveries.

Demi chef de partie
This is the next step up: running a station with more responsibilities. It is the time when the chefs prove themselves and show a willingness to learn and work.

Chef de partie
Literally 'head of a team', the next full rank up with the authority to organise other chefs. This is a managerial step up. In a small restaurant a chef de partie may be in charge of just one chef. The duties could include staff meals, sauces, meat and fish prep, and hot starters.

Sous chef
This is the head chef's immediate number two who is capable of doing the head chef's job in their absence. In a larger kitchen there may be a junior or senior sous chef, in a smaller one just the sous (under or sub) chef. In a big

kitchen, the sous chef manages and does very little cooking. This is a position of authority. A junior sous chef is part chef, part manager.

Head chef

In any kitchen the head chef is in charge. Their only superior is the executive head chef who may be in charge of several restaurants, either independent ones or those within a large establishment, such as a hotel. In a small restaurant, the head chef is responsible for all the cooking, ordering, management and training.

The head chef's jobs are to create menus, write the recipes or guidelines to go with the recipes, to find the best suppliers, and to recruit, discipline and promote staff. In the absence of a sous chef, they are also responsible for rotas, for giving out specific jobs (such as larder work, cleaning, cooking, management) and for making sure the kitchen is up to scratch for hygiene and health inspections.

They are also responsible for reporting to the overall management, for discussing future strategies, for any special holiday catering (such as Christmas or weddings), banqueting, dealing with customer and staff issues and stock-taking checks. Liaison with front-of-house staff may be delegated to the sous chef.

THE KITCHEN CAREER

Working in a restaurant kitchen can take many directions. For a commis chef with a goal, working under a good head chef is a period of learning. A commis working in a small restaurant is part of an equally small brigade, and they will work in all stations. They will learn more quickly – and better – if the head chef is good and is eager to pass on their knowledge and expertise. In a large restaurant, a commis chef might find things more daunting due to the sheer numbers in the kitchen and will stay only if treated well.

The best way to learn about the restaurant business is to be a commis in a good, small restaurant with perhaps four or five chefs and being involved in all stages of the cooking. It is, therefore, of paramount importance to find commis chefs who are willing to learn and who are committed to the job, particularly in small and medium-sized restaurants.

It is usually not financially viable to have several chefs of the same ranking unless business is booming. Hence the importance of a keen (and less well paid) commis chef. But do look beyond cooking skills when interviewing for this position: the right attitude is of equal importance.

Women chefs

There's a myth that women aren't strong enough to get on in the kitchen – that they cry a lot, can't lift heavy stock pots, can't stand the pace and are easily flustered. While women may still have a great deal to prove, witness head chefs Sally Clarke (Clarke's), Angela Hartnett (Murano), Ruth Rogers and Rose Gray (River Café), Samantha Clark (Moro), Helena Poulakka (Sonny's), all in London, Sonia Brooke-Little (Churchill Arms, Paxford, Gloucestershire), and Shirley Spear and Isobel Tomlin (the Three Chimneys, Isle of Skye). These represent some of the many excellent women head chefs in Britain.

TEAM WORKING

The manager is responsible for making sure the kitchen and front-of-house staff work together as a team, or at least for recognising the tensions between these two groups and for settling their disputes and grievances.

The old adage that the customer is always right may not apply to food. When food is ready it is at its peak condition and should be served immediately, not when the customer wishes to vacate their seat at the bar. This is where skilled waiting comes in. The waiter is the person who seats the customer and who is aware of the order of priority in the kitchen. The waiter judges the timing of each table and reports back to the kitchen if diners are taking an inordinate amount of time over the first course, for example, or if faster service is required.

There should be mutual respect between your kitchen and front-of-house staff. If the latter doesn't understand the former's work patterns and skill in putting each dish together, then trust, confidence and communication will break down.

This is where management comes in. The manager should be sensitive to the atmosphere between the kitchen and restaurant. Turn the tables now and then and get them to perform each other's work, or let the different sections shadow each other so that they understand each other's challenges and difficulties.

DRESS CODE, BEHAVIOUR AND COMMUNICATING WITH CUSTOMERS

Your front-of-house staff should reflect the kind of restaurant you are running, so make sure of the following.

Appearance

If your staff have a uniform, this should be clean, pressed and well fitting. If you operate a no-uniform policy, then stipulate what your staff should wear and be vigilant. Also stipulate what type of shoes they should wear, that these should be in good repair and should be cleaned regularly. Have a policy on wearing jewellery, make-up and style of hair.

Hygiene

All staff should have short, clean, unvarnished nails and *must* wash their hands after a break, going to the loo, returning to duty after going to the shops, handling stock from a van, etc.

All the above also applies to kitchen staff. The cleanliness of their aprons and the chef's jackets and the wearing of head gear are of paramount importance, not only to the overall standards of hygiene but also if seen by your customers, who will judge your restaurant accordingly.

Smoking

Smoking was banned on 1 July 2007 in restaurants and other publics areas. This means that your staff are equally banned from smoking on the premises and must use an outside area you have designated. Make sure that smokers are not seen by your customers because this really does give the wrong impression (see page 22 for the full legislation).

All smokers should wash their hands before service. If there is an all-pervading smell of smoking, this can be a real turn-off for your customers (smoky clothes and breath). But banning smoking is tantamount to calling for a mutiny. You may be fortunate enough to employ non-smokers but, if not, be vigilant.

Drugs

If you suspect any staff member has a drug problem (for example, if they come in late, don't turn up at all or show signs of drug and alcohol abuse), deal with it immediately.

Music

Music is often turned up for the benefit of staff who seemingly can't live without it. Your staff will also bring in their own music to inflict on your customers if you aren't vigilant. Don't let this happen because it can spiral out of control and will soon be seen as a 'right'. If your customers can't make themselves heard, they will vote with their feet.

Meeting and greeting

Meeting and greeting has to be well pitched. The customer should preferably be met at the door and shown to a table once the staff have found out if they have booked or whether they wish to book or make an enquiry.

Do your staff speak English or the language of your restaurant? Can they communicate effectively without that language?

Your staff should on no account gather in groups by the bar and ignore the door opening or continue to carry on a personal conversation. This is too often the case, and the customer is not made to feel welcome or wanted. Your staff should at least say hello to the customer. In Britain this seems to be a difficulty. Slamming the menu down in front of the customer and asking in a bored voice what they would like to drink is very off-putting. Instead, the staff should look them in the eye, smile, offer a greeting, ask where they would like to sit if this is an option, offer them a menu immediately and find out if they would like a drink or wait until they have chosen from the menu. This will make your customers feel at ease.

Service

A good waiting staff member is able to understand each table's needs: business tables, loving couples' tables or a family outing all need different approaches. Self-respect and respect for others are paramount, as are professionalism and efficiency. A good memory is also important.

Make sure your waiting staff know what is on the menu and if there are any specials they can describe, but not in a fast monotone. No one will take this in, with the result that your specials won't sell.

Your waiting staff should not only be aware of what the dishes consist of but also of wines by the glass, their types and which food they go with. They should also be knowledgeable about all the drinks on offer. What kind of coffee do you serve? What brandies are there?

The waiting staff should also make sure there is sufficient space on the table before serving plates, vegetables, wine bottles, butter, bread and other items. It's no good just pushing things around the table to fit them in because this creates tension with the customer and a feeling of not being looked after appropriately.

When it comes to the bill, the waiting staff should be aware of people's needs. They should watch their body language and ask if they would like anything more. They should not buzz off into the kitchen to chat up the sous chef.

Lasting impressions: some dos and don'ts

Your staff should say goodbye as warmly as they greeted the customers. This will create a lasting impression. People don't just go to restaurants for a good meal: they go for a good time out, a pleasing atmosphere, good service. No one should be over-familiar, loud, noisy or rude. Everyone should be friendly, pleasant, efficient and professional. Enjoy yourself, but leave the background music alone. It's not your party, it's theirs.

Tips for professional waiting skills:

☐ When seating three people at a table for four, for example, always remove the place setting of cutlery, glasses, side plate and napkin for where a fourth person may have sat. This applies to any table size when all the seats aren't taken up.

☐ Hold a plate by placing four fingers under it, the thumb on the side and not on the surface of the plate.

☐ Serve from the left and remove from the right.

☐ When holding two plates in one hand, balance one plate on the forearm by the wrist, the other underneath with three fingers under the second plate, thumb and small finger on the rim.

☐ Clear plates, the stronger part of the forearm and wrist should bear the weight.

☐ Serve drinks on the right where the glass is positioned.

☐ Serve food without asking 'who's having the paté?' Identify each diner by number, starting perhaps with the one nearest to the bar as number one, then going around clockwise.

☐ Orders must be written legibly, preferably in capitals, so that your kitchen staff can readily identify each dish.

☐ Always add any other information (e.g. 'medium-rare') clearly, the number of covers, the waiting staff member's name and table number.

☐ Always hold glasses by their stem, never by the bowl, unless clearing dirty glasses.

☐ Clear the table after each course, leaving it set for the next course.

□ Always make sure the table is left cleared ready for dessert or
coffee, removing the salt and pepper and unnecessary cutlery.

□ Clear plates only when everyone at a table has finished
eating. It gives the wrong impression (i.e. you're hurrying
them) if cleared at different times, putting the slow eater in
a dilemma.

MANAGEMENT SKILLS

A good manager has self-confidence and a complete understanding of the
operation. They also have a good rapport with the kitchen and restaurant staff
and possess charm. They are leaders, take responsibility and can delegate well
but must also be able to be hands-on without undermining other staff (e.g.
showing them up before customers and other staff members). The same dos
and don'ts apply to the manager as to the waiting staff (see above).

The manager has ultimate control over the reservations and should plan each
session successfully: delegating changes of seating to the waiting staff to suit a
particular party, noting special requirements and informing the staff of these
requirements. The manager should be able to set up a table plan of the whole
restaurant and should number each table. It is essential to achieve the
maximum table take-up. This is a skill that comes with practice.

They should maintain a clear booking plan, with spaces for names, numbers of
covers, times, table numbers, contact telephone numbers and any special
requirements or comments about the booking. They should liaise with the chef
about how many customers can be booked in at a specific time (e.g. 8 pm when
the restaurant is at its most hectic) or about how many other tables can be
accommodated if large parties are booked in. Balancing time and space is the key.

Make sure that all your staff write bookings in a legible way and that they all
know how to take bookings.

 Lead by example. Train all your staff to respect their work and
the contribution they make to your restaurant.

STAFF ROTAS

Rotas are vital. They enable everyone, at a glance, to see who is working or absent. They can be made up on a weekly basis but, with good management, they can be worked out four weeks in advance, taking into consideration holidays, days off, staff shortages, overtime and busy times of the year when more staff will be required. Include your managers in the rota to demonstrate that all staff are equal and accountable.

It is important to put your or your chef's managerial skills into practice and to be as fair to all your staff members as possible. For example, unless specifically asked for, don't pile all the evening work on certain staff members. Give them the same number of day shifts as their co-workers so they can have a night off with their family and friends.

Discuss the rota with all your staff and follow up any complaints or dissatisfaction promptly because grievances can build up.

 Include cleaning and refrigeration-temperature checking on staff rotas so that these are emphasised. These tasks should be seen as a necessary part of the working week, not just something to be fitted in as and when or done in a desultory fashion or even forgotten.

Print out staff rotas and preferably reprint them if there are a number of changes so there is no confusion. Otherwise a staff member may not turn up, mistakenly thinking they had swapped duties.

On page 132 is an example of a staff rota for a small restaurant that is closed on Mondays. The sous chef takes over the chef's work on Thursdays and these roles are reversed on Tuesdays. There may also be more part-time waiting staff. If the owner were in charge of the management, they would be present most if not all days, but not necessarily all hours.

Staff	Tuesday	Wednesday	Thursday	Friday	Saturday	Sunday	
Head chef	8–2 pm 6–11 pm	10–2 pm 6–11 pm	Off	9–2 pm 6–11 pm	10–2 pm 6–11 pm	10–4	pm
Sous chef	Off	10–2 pm 6–11 pm	9–2 pm 6–11 pm	10–2 pm 6–11 pm	10–2 pm 6–11 pm	10–4	pm
KP 1*	9–5 pm	5–11 pm	5–11 pm	9–5 pm	5–11 pm	Off	
KP 2*	5–11 pm	Off	9–5 pm	5–11 pm	9–5 pm	9–5	pm
Waiter 1	Off	10–2 pm 6–11 pm	10–2 pm	6–11 pm	10–2 pm 6–11 pm	11–5	pm
Waiter 2	10–2 pm 6–11 pm	Off	6–11 pm	10–2 pm 6–11 pm	10–2 pm 6–11 pm	11 – 5	pm

* Will also perform cleaning duties in the kitchen, restaurant, toilets.

Cleaning tips

Cleaning is an essential part of any food business. It minimises the risk of food contamination and infestation and provides a pleasant and safe working environment.

To be effective, cleaning must be planned and incorporated into the staff rota:

☐ When preparing food, adopt a clean-as-you-go policy with spillages and food debris.

☐ Draw up a list of all items of equipment and areas for cleaning and how often they need to be cleaned.

☐ Compile a separate list for toilet maintenance and cleaning.

☐ What materials and equipment should be used for equipment and areas?

☐ Who is responsible for these jobs?

☐ Prepare a comprehensive scheduled programme.

☐ Review the programme if a new piece of equipment or a new area comes into being.

☐ Store cleaning materials away from all food.

☐ Keep cleaning materials in their original containers.

☐ Don't mix cleaning materials because they can give off noxious fumes.

☐ Never clean an area that is still being used by customers with bleach or other strong-smelling cleaners as the odour is extremely off-putting.

☐ If strong cleaning smells linger on after opening times, find another type of cleaning agent because customers really do dislike a hospital-type smell and may not stay – or return.

☐ Wash hands after using any cleaning materials.

9

DESIGNING MENUS

The menu is the restaurant's raison d'être, the pulling power that brings people in. Watch people around a menu outside a restaurant's door: they are weighing up the pros and cons of crossing the threshold. They will have noticed the many attractions before them: the use of space, the décor, the staff, lighting and the atmosphere. What determines their final decision? The menu.

THE IMPORTANCE OF THE MENU

Menus showcase your kitchen's abilities and strengths. They represent the coming together of the restaurateur, chef, supplier and style of the restaurant. Your menu is hugely important not only because of its content but also in the way it is set out.

To maximise your profit, put your higher-priced items second from the top and second from the bottom because customers tend to order more often from these two locations. When reviewing your menu, remove dishes that don't sell. You don't want any dish that does not pull its weight.

FOOD CONSISTENCY

The food has to be consistent. Your customers will leave you in droves if the food on their plates doesn't match the last meals they enjoyed in your restaurant. If standards are allowed to slip – you hire a chef who likes to create a buzz but who can't do a good job day in day out – then you must re-examine your kitchen's strengths.

If you offer complex food, there is more chance that it will go wrong. Simplicity, therefore, is the best way forward, unless you have an exceptionally talented chef who is able to concoct the finest food on a daily basis without a hitch.

But even simplicity demands care and attention to detail. Just throwing a whole lot of good ingredients together without a knowledge of food marriages will result in a horrid mishmash of tastes and ill-judged flavours.

The menu war of the sexes

Guy Browning wrote in the *Guardian Weekend*: '… women start at the bottom of a menu and work up. They look for death by chocolate, then justify the end of the meal by seeking out the most lettuce-rich dish at the beginning. Men start in the middle, where they look for the word "sausage". Once they've found that, they can safely locate something that is deep-fried and as far as possible from the words "goat's cheese".

'It takes three reads of a menu to get ordering right: the first to find the sausages; the second to see if there's an interesting alternative; and while your partner is ordering, that last, desperate scan to locate the sausages.

'Never ask what's good: it's all good. And don't ask what they recommend. They'll recommend the leathery old monkfish that they've been trying to shift since Monday. Only have the monkfish if they recommend the sausages.'

CREATING A MENU

To create a menu, it is vital that your head chef knows and understands these basic principles: produce, combinations, how to cook them and the customer base.

The chef Nico Ladenis, in his *My Gastronomy* cookbook, says that 'perfection is the result of simplicity. That is my philosophy: to be restrained in presentation, to produce each dish consistently and always approaching the ideal'.

His own culinary marriages made in heaven include:

☐ duck and orange;

☐ salmon and sorrel;

☐ strawberries and cream;

☐ steak and chips;

- ☐ tomatoes and basil;

- ☐ chicken with tarragon;

- ☐ cold lobster with mayonnaise;

- ☐ lamb and garlic;

- ☐ fried eggs and bacon;

- ☐ foie gras and Sauternes; and

- ☐ chicken and morels.

I would add steak with a Béarnaise sauce, fish soup with rouille, asparagus with Hollandaise, salmon with a beurre blanc sauce, pork loin with crackling and real apple sauce, lamb with couscous, tiger prawns with Thai ingredients, caviar and chilled vodka. And fish and chips, roast Mediterranean vegetables with goat's cheese, the best cheeses with appropriate bread and wine, bread-and-butter pudding made with brioche bread and a first-class crème anglaise.

Nico's philosophy on food is one of simplicity of approach followed by the use of perfect ingredients. According to him, there should be no marriage between meat and shellfish or shellfish and fruit, sound principles to go by. Duck and lobster, duck and papaya, lobster and mango, beef with Cointreau and mango (seen on one menu recently), crab and beef are just some examples that do not sit comfortably together in one dish.

The things that make a good chef are knowing:

- ☐ how to create a simple dish perfectly;

- ☐ how to cook a steak or fish faultlessly;

- ☐ how to time a dish; and

- ☐ when to cook each dish to order and in what order.

Garnishing your food

Be wary of over-elaboration. Some chefs consider garnish as adding a touch of sophistication to their dishes. Instead, it adds confusion and unnecessary clutter to the plate. What does a slice of orange have to do with a crispy duck and puy lentil salad or a fillet steak? More is less and never more so than on a plate. Food should look like food, not some fanciful concoction.

USING FIRST-RATE PRODUCE

If your chef sources second-rate produce it won't taste any better if served on the finest china or the best, whitest linen. Nor will expensive carpets or décor help to disguise the fact that the establishment is overcharging for poor food. Good, honest restaurateurs will go out of their way to source the best produce available. This doesn't mean flying in duck from Paraguay or caviar from the Caspian.

☐ Find carrots that have flavour and cook them with interest and knowledge.

☐ Locate a free-range chicken that really tastes like chicken and not blotting paper.

☐ Track down very well hung beef of note.

☐ Buy good-quality chocolate with high cocoa solids for the best chocolate tart.

☐ Find a herb specialist who will supply French tarragon, not flavourless Russian tarragon.

☐ Source the basics with understanding and passion: bread, butter, coffee, wine.

Don't look for difficulty. If certain produce is not available or is tricky to obtain on a regular basis, don't put that dish on your menu. Chefs must have peace of mind when ordering to fulfil a menu's promise.

WHAT TO COOK AND WHY TO COOK IT

Cook what you like eating yourself and you will be halfway there. But if you have a narrow palate you may be in the wrong job! Don't cook what you don't understand. If you understand and find pleasure in cooking imaginative vegetarian food, make this your forte or learn how to cook other dishes outside your repertoire.

Women chefs tend to like cooking food they understand; they like to give pleasure via the table. It is a huge buzz doing just this, to which I and many other women chefs can testify. Many male chefs have the notion that they have to show off. Why?

Alice Waters, the remarkable and much-loved Californian restaurateur who started the trend of looking for the best produce and cooking this simply (and if she couldn't find it she grew it) is reported to have said:

I opened a restaurant so that people could come and eat; remember that the final goal is to nourish and nurture those who gather at your table. It is there, within this nurturing process, that I have found the greatest satisfaction and sense of accomplishment.

Menu planning and dish creation

Planning a menu is an essential part of eating well. Professional chefs plan their menus with care, taking into account tastes, fashions, health, seasonal food, limitations of time, budget and practicality. Choosing a wine list to go with your food is equally important. A balanced menu is a must.

When compiling ideas for your menu, look first at what you want to achieve, whom you wish to attract to your restaurant, what the kitchen can handle in terms of staff numbers, ability and equipment, and the cost to produce each dish.

Many chefs have a germ of an idea in their minds when creating new dishes. Talking to people, reading about dishes in the restaurant guides, in newspapers and magazines, and seeing dishes created on television by the likes of Gary Rhodes, Rick Stein, Nigella Lawson, Jamie Oliver and Delia Smith may spark off an idea.

It pays to think each idea through thoroughly before putting it on the menu:

☐ How much prepping will this dish require? Can it be costed out favourably enough to put on the menu?

☐ Where do the ingredients come from?

☐ Does it fit into the existing menu or does it upset the balance of fish, meat, vegetarian and sweet dishes?

Menu balance

Look at the number of cheese/fish/pork or chicken dishes. Too many similar dishes? Think about the range of coloured dishes (too many browns and beiges), of dishes with dairy produce and dishes containing chilli. Is there a great deal of fried food or three types of the ubiquitous salmon?

Nico himself didn't ask this question of balance often enough. One menu of his I recall showed his fondness for offal. His customers had to negotiate kidneys, liver, foie gras and sweetbreads, with little else on offer. Sometimes even the great ones can get it wrong.

Questions to ask yourself when working out a menu

It can take several years of cooking in a professional kitchen to reach the stage of knowing instinctively what will and what won't work in your kitchen. But don't let your creative process be stilted by fear or indecision. Try out your ideas, present them to your team and ask them for their opinions.

You could also try them out on good customers who will welcome an opportunity to be of use and be flattered by being asked. In the early days of putting a menu together, you can easily waste money and time. The questions that need answering include the following:

- ☐ Is it a worthwhile dish to develop?

- ☐ Are the ingredients available?

- ☐ What would my gross profit be on this dish?

- ☐ Does it keep well or may there be high wastage?

- ☐ Does it present well?

- ☐ How does it fit in with other dishes on the menu?

- ☐ Can I delegate other chefs to do this dish in my absence or are the skills in my current brigade?

Never make drastic changes to your menu. Change it gradually and according to the season. Your customers may be upset by too drastic a menu change.

A good chef simply cannot create dozens of new dishes at once because perfection, or near-perfection, will be lost. Fine-tuning a dish takes time. If, on the other hand, you are doing an assembly job – putting the best smoked salmon you can find on the menu or oysters or a fine ham with a chicory salad – then little fine tuning is required. The dish can go on the menu straightaway.

When creating a new menu, pay attention to the number of hot and cold starters. If you include too many hot ones, you will slow down the process of getting food out quickly to your hungry, impatient customers. Achieving this balance is very important.

MENU AND DRINK PRICING

The aim of pricing is to achieve the best profits and to ensure the long-term success of your business. So you need to think about the following:

- ☐ What type of customers you will have and what they can pay.

- ☐ What quality of produce you will buy.

- ☐ What standards of cooking will be achieved.

- ☐ What the standards of service and comfort are in your restaurant.

- ☐ What the competition is like.

- ☐ What your plans are for the future.

Initally you may wish to keep your prices down to attract customers. The danger with this is that, when they become aware of the price rises, your customers may decamp elsewhere because they can no longer afford to dine with you. This is an area that needs flair combined with a good business sense.

 On average, restaurateurs should aim to have a 60–70 per cent profit on food and a 60 per cent profit on wines.

CREATING CONTENTED CUSTOMERS

The food should be at the right temperature. Do you fiddle about trying to create a tower of jumbled ingredients, the food becoming colder by the second? Or do you simply present your food on the plate, dressing it minimally if at all and then promptly serving it to the customer? Avoid food being returned because it is too cold. You will most assuredly have to cook it again from scratch, thereby creating waste and lowering your gross profit, to say nothing of alienating your customers.

Make sure you serve the wine, bread and water smartly. This will make your customers more relaxed. Aim to serve the first course within ten minutes of the order being placed, fifteen minutes maximum. People may walk out if the half hour is breached. Keep your customers informed if there is a delay. This is appreciated. Offer them more bread or a free glass of wine to keep them sweet. That is why it is so important to have a good selection of cold starters if your restaurant's pace is fast.

There is nothing new under the sun when it comes to creating new dishes – it's all just reinvention. But with top-class ingredients and good cooking, your food will stand out.

Tasting what you put on the menu

Good chefs always taste. One young chef I interviewed for my chefs' column arrogantly told me that he didn't need to taste the food he cooked because he had tasted it once and 'that was enough'. A good chef always tastes. That ice cream may need more vanilla or coffee, or the prawn and coconut dish could do with some more chilli.

Good communication between kitchen and front of house

Good chefs always discuss each new dish with the waiting staff so that they can talk to the customers with knowledge and are able to sell it effectively. If your staff shrug their shoulders or say 'I'll just ask the chef what's in this dish', this will create a bad impression, to say the least. There must be harmony and communication between cook and server.

The *Automobile Association Guide's* ten top tips for better restaurant cooking

1. Source your suppliers carefully. Demand the best and only serve the best.

2. Use local produce where possible – if it's good enough.

3. Have one eye on the seasons – although most foods are available all year round, they nevertheless tend to be at their best for only one season.

4. Cook real food from whole raw ingredients.

5. Keep it simple, be true to the ingredients. Don't be creative just for the sake of it.

6. Always question – how can I improve this dish?

7. Taste the food you create. And remember the diner is eating more than just a forkful – so as a plateful, will it be too much, too heavy, too rich, or just plain boring?

8. Keep a sense of balance. Don't overcook, don't undercook, don't over-sauce, don't under-sauce, don't under-season. This sounds really basic, but it's where many meals fail.

9. Eat out. Get to know what the competition's doing.

10. Don't cook for accolades. The best food comes from a kitchen that has confidence in its own ability, where the chef is in tune with the needs of the restaurant's customer base.

WRITING AND COMPILING THE MENU

If your menu is written in flowery language – 'puddles of chive essence', 'a mosaic of', 'a symphony of', 'multitudes of coulis' – this may put your customers off instantly. What is a 'chef's special'? Something the kitchen has too much of and is desperate to shift?

Don't use an over-the-top handwriting style. Similarly, many fast-food, 'family' restaurants have menus that are confusing and very, very long. But by analysing these you may find that most of the ingredients turn up time and time again under a different guise. Rather like Chinese menus.

☐ Choose a font that is clear if you are printing the menus in-house.

☐ Make your headings succinct and clear.

☐ State clearly any extras.

☐ Avoid too many supplements on a *table d' hôte* (set) menu. It might as well be an *à la carte* if they are piled on.

☐ Tone down the descriptions.

☐ There is no need to add all the ingredients because this will confuse. The reader will have to return to many dishes again and again to remind themselves of their contents.

On page 144 is a sample past menu from a Welsh-Italian restaurant which, although it is succinct and clear, the balance is somewhat questionable.

The balance is upset by pancetta in two of the four starters and with more pork in another starter. All four have a meat content. Breadcrumbs are found in two of the eight dishes and more bread comes in the form of bread-and-butter pudding for dessert.

The majority of dishes are on the heavy, filling side, not in keeping with today's lighter food. The ice creams will need explaining to each customer unless they know Italian. On the plus side, it does state that the kitchen makes its own food and sources local produce.

Types of menus

There are two types of menu, the *table d' hôte* (table of the host), known more familiarly as the set menu, and the *à la carte* (from the card). The main difference between the two is that the *à la carte* has differently priced dishes, whereas the *table d' hôte* has an inclusive price for the whole meal.

The *carte du jour* (literally, card of the day) is not very common these days and offers a fixed meal with one or more courses for a set price. A *prix fixe* (fixed price) menu is similar. Sometimes the price also includes a glass of wine or a substitute drink.

Lunch Menu

TWO COURSES £16.95
THREE COURSES £19.95

STARTERS

Leek and potato soup with pancetta

Salad of endive, pancetta, shaved fennel, dolcelatte and rocket

Home made terrine of wild Welsh rabbit with marrow chutney

Crispy, breadcrumb belly pork with lemon, capers and fennel

MAIN COURSES

Home made venison sausages with mashed potatoes, greens and onion gravy

Home made breadcrumbed fish cake with caesar salad

Braised shoulder of local lamb with rosemary potatoes and greens

Anna's lasagne bolognese

DESSERTS

Home made gelati and sorbetti

Gelati: gianduia, fior de latte, tutti frutti, stacciatella

Sorbetti: blackcurrant, wimberry, pear and saffron

Vanilla pannacotta with bramley apple and raison compote and cinnamon crumble

Panetonne bread and butter pudding

Hot chocolate fondant with praline ice cream

The *table d' hôte* or *prix fixe* menu (set menu):

☐ A menu with a fixed number of courses.

☐ Limited choice within each course or no choice.

☐ The price is fixed.

☐ The food is usually available at a set time, say between 6 and 7.30 pm.

The *à la carte* menu:

☐ The choice is larger than the *table d' hôte*.

☐ Each dish is priced separately.

☐ Each dish is generally cooked to order. The waiting time may be longer.

The advantage for the customer of the *table d'hôte* or *prix fixe* menu is that there are no hidden charges. The disadvantage is that the portions may be smaller. The disadvantage to the restaurateur is forecasting how many dishes to prepare. Too many will lead to wastage. To avoid this, keep the food as simple as possible. For example, add a Roquefort and bacon salad to the starter list rather than a salmon and avocado terrine, because the latter is more in keeping with an *à la carte* menu. The salad is easy and quick to prepare and the wastage is minimal.

If you run out of prepared dishes, be prepared to offer a more expensive dish with less profit. Therefore, keep the set menu simple, easy to prepare and inexpensive so that all the dishes can be quickly and effectively prepped to order.

Tips for menus
To make your menus work:

☐ Choose your ingredients seasonally.

☐ Choose lighter food for summer and more substantial food for winter, including fashionable comfort food.

☐ Have a good balance of fish, meat, vegetables, cheeses and desserts. For example, have beef, lamb, chicken, offal, fish and vegetarian dishes plus fruit-based, chocolate-based and cream-based desserts.

☐ Bear in mind that beef is expensive, so this may end up as your loss-leader. You will have a better gross profit if your staff can steer people towards other dishes.

☐ Include a selection of plainly cooked food, such as grilled salmon or a light salad, or be able to offer it should it be asked for.

☐ Have a balance of hot and cold food.

☐ Ask your staff to introduce customers to the more adventurous food on the menu. This may work in a small restaurant but it may not be practical in a large one.

☐ Change the menu not only for the sake of the customer but also for the chef's sake. They mustn't become bored. This is when standards can slip.

☐ Recognise dishes that don't sell and remove them from the menu to save wastage and your gross profit falling.

☐ Your specials board can reflect your buying prowess. If offered some good-value fresh fish by a trusted supplier on the day, put it on the specials board.

☐ Avoid putting on past its sell by date food on the specials board. Learn to see ahead if some items aren't selling quickly enough and then put them on that board. But don't jeopardise your business by trying to off-load going-off food.

☐ Discuss the menu in detail with your kitchen staff and ask for their input.

☐ Don't even think about putting something on the menu just because it looks pretty. It has to taste great too.

☐ Be wary of following fashions. You may end up with a mishmash of dishes that the kitchen can't cope with and that are far removed from the genuine article. Good, authentic sushi is an example.

☐ Be creative with the trimmings and leftovers. Will fish trimmings make a good fishcake for the specials board? Will cheeses not fit to be seen on the cheese board, due to their miniscule size, be good for stuffing peppers with tomatoes and tapenade as a special?

☐ You can afford to be ambiguous with something as specialised as game because its availability might suddenly dry up. Substitution is the only way forward. 'Game in season served in the traditional way, according to availability' might be an option.

☐ The advantage of having the menu written up (clearly) on a blackboard in a small restaurant is that, if supplies run out of a certain vital ingredient, such as salmon, you wipe it off the board.

◻ If you're not making a profit, you will have to make changes. Ask for prices from another supplier or, if you can, find the same quality from another source by bypassing the middleman.

◻ One method many chefs use is to add £1 or so on to the best-selling dishes. Your profit could be on track again.

ACCOMODATING SPECIAL DIETS

You will almost certainly have to deal with special diets for people with allergies, who are diabetic, for those who want a low-cholesterol diet or for those who are following a low-salt regime.

Generally speaking, those with medical conditions or who just want to follow strict eating guidelines will know what they can and can't eat. If the customer explains to a staff member that they are avoiding a particular ingredient, it is important for that staff member to find out from the chef if the diner's choice avoids these items.

Allergies

Allergies can include the gluten in wheat, rye and barley. This allergy is known as coeliac. Other allergies include peanuts and all their derivatives, sesame seeds, cashews, pecans, brazils and walnuts, as well as milk, fish, shellfish and eggs.

Diabetic

In those with diabetes, the body is unable to control the level of glucose in the blood. Diets may include avoiding high sugar dishes and some of those from the cholesterol list below.

Low cholesterol

A low-cholesteral diet involves the avoidance of polyunsaturated fats and limited amounts of animal fats. Food that can be eaten includes lean meat, fish, fruit and vegetables, plus low-fat milk, cheese and yoghurt.

Low salt (or sodium)

This diet involves a reduction of salt in the cooking or no salt at all.

Cultural and religious dietary requirements

As our culture becomes more diverse, it may help to be aware of the differing requirements of certain faiths and of the ways of cooking that are allowed.

Muslims:

No meat, offal or animal fat unless it is halal meat (as required by Islamic dietary law).

Jews:

☐ No pork or pork products.

☐ No shellfish.

☐ No animal fats or gelatine from animals considered to be unclean or not slaughtered according to the prescribed manner.

☐ Restrictions on methods of preparation and cooking practices.

☐ The preparation and eating of meat and dairy produce at the same meal is not allowed.

Sikhs:

☐ No beef or pork.

☐ No halal meat.

☐ May prefer a vegetarian diet.

Hindhus:

☐ No beef.

☐ Rarely pork.

☐ Some Hindhus will not eat any other meats, fish or eggs.

Vegans:

☐ No food of any animal origin.

☐ Vegans will eat: vegetables, vegetable oils, cereals, fruits and seeds.

INSTRUCTING YOUR KITCHEN STAFF ON FOLLOWING YOUR RECIPES

The head chef is responsible for teaching the staff how to cook recipes devised by them in an abbreviated, professional way. These recipes are a kind of shorthand, a checklist of ingredients and method, a variety of pointers rather than the usual recipe of full measurements found in cookbooks.

Develop a card system or file the recipes on a computer. Then you will always be able to find the required recipe at short notice to give it to a new chef who may not have cooked the dish before or who is not familiar with your method. Compile a master file in which each recipe is stored under a heading, such as soups (hot and cold), salads (warm and cold), chicken, fish, beef, lamb, liver and so on. For desserts you could have sub-headings, such as ice creams, English puddings, fruit tarts, dairy desserts, pastries and basic preparations, such as proper custard and chocolate sauce.

Add the date when the dish was put on the menu, where the original recipe came from and its page if from a cookbook. Cross-indexing is also helpful (e.g. lemon-based recipes). Add notes to recipes if they have been modified (the temperature has been changed, the type of chocolate giving the best results or how many servings each recipe yields). For ease of teaching, stick to either the metric or imperial system. This will simplify work in the kitchen.

Example of long recipe and its shortened version

Apple tart on puff pastry with a caramel sauce: for two

4 golden delicious dessert apples, peeled, halved and cored

2 thin rounds of puff pastry 15 cm in diameter, placed on a baking sheet, and pricked with a fork to prevent rising

10 g caster sugar

knob of butter

sugar syrup (see recipe card)

caramel sauce (see recipe card)

1. Pre-heat the oven to 170°C. Cut the apples into very thin slices and arrange around the pastry in a circle, starting at the edge and working towards the centre.

2. Sprinkle the apples with sugar then dot with the butter.

3. Bake for around 10–15 minutes or until the base is cooked and light brown. If the apples have not caramelised well place under a grill or

salamander, covering the edges of the pastry so that they don't burn. Or use a blow torch.

4. Glaze with the sugar syrup and serve with several tablespoonfuls of caramel sauce.

The reduced version

Apple tart recipe: for two

4 apples, peeled, cored and cut thinly

2 rounds of puff pastry

caster sugar

butter

sugar syrup (see recipe card)

caramel sauce (see recipe card)

Put apple slices on pastry in circles, sprinkle with sugar, add butter. Bake in 170 ºC oven until browned and caramelised. Continue with blow torch if necessary. Glaze with sugar syrup. Garnish with caramel sauce.

10

CHOOSING SUPPLIERS

No matter how brilliant a chef is, they cannot cook good food if the produce sourced is cheap and nasty. Because food is increasingly being prepared simply rather than being sauced, the ingredients are given centre stage. *Your food will be judged on its quality.* Therefore, choose your suppliers with the utmost care. Work out your gross profit with quality at the forefront of all your calculations. Search for excellent meat, a good supplier of game and fish, and top-notch vegetables and fruit. Don't skimp on anything, not even the salt and pepper you cook with and place on the table.

LOOKING FOR KEY SUPPLIERS

Your bread is vital: this sets your restaurant's tone because it may be the first mouthful a customer has. There is a now plethora of suppliers in Britain and Ireland of dried goods, such as olive oils, olives and all manner of specialist foods. Or you could import directly from a company abroad. Go to food fairs, events and exhibitions locally and in the major cities to track down the best produce. Talk to other restaurateurs. Most will be only too willing to pass on good suppliers, and those to avoid.

Obtain price lists, ask for samples and bargain – ask for wholesale prices. Consider buying by mail order. Consult *Yellow Pages* for other sources and go on the web to locate cheese and other specialist companies. Cross the channel to buy more cheaply if you're in the south of England. But always think quality: ask to taste anything before buying it. This is normal in France!

If you can, visit Borough Market, Borough Street, London, SE1 near London Bridge (0207) 407 1002 (www.boroughmarket.org.uk) for a shortcut to finding superb produce. Contact Covent Garden Market in London (www.Conventgardenlondonuk.com) and major fruit and vegetable markets in your area for suppliers.

WORKING WITH YOUR SUPPLIERS

Once you have narrowed down your suppliers and have started buying from them, always check your supplies, sending back anything that doesn't have quality stamped all over it (in the nicest possible way, of course), so establishing an excellent working relationship with them. This way they will look after you and will bend over backwards to keep your business. Always query any accounting error promptly and pay your bills on time.

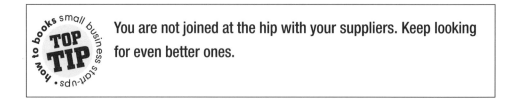

You are not joined at the hip with your suppliers. Keep looking for even better ones.

Suppliers will usually call you to find out what your order is, or you could call them. There is usually an after-hours ordering service to leave messages on for a next-day delivery.

Tips for buying:

☐ Always serve the freshest fish. Once it's past its best, throw it away.

☐ Game is gaining in popularity thanks to its healthy-eating tag. There is wild and farmed game. You could also try boar on your menu.

☐ Demand longer hanging for your beef, 28 days or over. Look out for darker-coloured, marbled meat.

☐ Insist on the best vegetables for their intense flavour. Go organic for tastier vegetables. Try different varieties. Respect seasons.

☐ It is worth doing some research to find really tasty fruit, apples in particular. Unfortunately, woolly peaches and dull apples and strawberries abound.

☐ Find a good cheese supplier – or three. Shop around for regional cheeses. Make sure your staff can identify the cheeses when serving them.

☐ There is some truly awful smoked salmon out there. Be discerning.

☐ Don't buy just any chocolate – source one with high cocoa solids.

☐ Coffee finishes off a good meal with character. Make sure yours is memorable. Source the best and invest in an espresso machine.

SOURCING LOCALLY

When I started as chef/restaurateur of Soanes, Petworth, West Sussex, in the 1980s, local produce sourcing was extremely limited. Excellent fish, vegetables and cheeses had to come from Covent Garden or Rungis, the Paris market.

Today's restaurateurs are spoilt for choice if they wish to source quality ingredients that are local, regional and seasonal. The added advantage is that this helps to cut food miles and, as a result, pollution and fuel consumption.

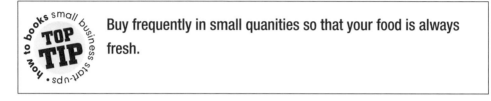

Buy frequently in small quanities so that your food is always fresh.

While there is a trend for better restaurateurs to offer locally or regionally sourced sausages, cheeses, meat, vegetables, fruit and drink, is this produce chosen with real care? It could be that the buying of local and regional food is merely paying lip service to current trends. Look for quality.

Does the customer really know or mind? There does seem to be a growing band of customers with high expectations who choose restaurants and pubs that celebrate the 'extra mile' travelled by the chef to source the best food around without the stabilisers, additives and other 'benefits' of mass-produced food.

As Sir Terence Conran once said: 'I want to eat the cuisine of the country, democratic food. I am passionately interested in the improvement of quality ingredients cooked simply.' Alice Waters, chef/owner of Chez Panisse in California, has developed a 60-strong network of mostly local farmers and ranchers whose dedication to sustainable agriculture assures her restaurant of a steady supply of fresh ingredients. Her set menu is based purely on seasonal produce. Conran's and Waters' passion for this 'democratic' food seems to have filtered through as a growing band of chefs and restaurateurs now realise the untold benefits to their business if they source the best produce in their regions.

Look at the food on the menus at the restaurants listed in *The Good Food Guide* and other comprehensive guides and you will notice an increase in provenance: Lincolnshire grey partridge, Goosenargh and Deben duck, Cumbrian fell-bred meat, Cotswolds, Nidderdale, Southdown, Wiltshire and organic Highgrove lamb, and Dales-bred beef smoked and cured in Yorkshire ale.

Some examples

The Weaver's Shed restaurant in West Yorkshire goes one step further. They produce their own chicken, duck, quails' eggs and vegetables. Co-chef, co-owner Stephen Jackson's father grows cavolo nero, kholrabi, leeks, salads, soft fruits and no less than 75 herbs and wild plants for the transformed woollen mill. The saving, Stephen reckons, is £200 a week off supplier bills, 'a sensible way of progressing and cooking within the seasons'.

Lawrence Murphy, chef/owner of Fat Olives in Emsworth, Hampshire, a brasserie-style restaurant, 'gets local rabbit and game and two guys fish for sea bass in the Solent for us'. The menu reflects this enthusiastic, innovative chef's local food, with sourcing that includes all vegetables and fruit in season.

The Star Inn at Harome, North Yorkshire, is a showcase of English-sourced food with most dishes markedly quoting the provenance (Yoadwarth Mill salmon, Whitby crab, North Sea lobster). Chef Andrew Pern is in the Alice Waters' mould, sourcing seasonal produce within his own village: 'We've set the benchmark in the area with healthy competition from other pubs and restaurants upping the game. It's in everyone's interests.' The facts speak for themselves: over 1,000 people eat here a week.

At the other end of the sourcing scale comes Peter Gordon, the New Zealand co-chef/co-owner of London's Providores, a restaurant of fusions. 'I treat the world's culinary resources as one huge and exciting larder,' Peter says. The eclectic menu covers a huge range, from Exmoor-sourced duck, New Zealand venison and Suffolk Cross lamb to pomegranate molasses ('now available here thanks to its exposure'), plantains, tomatillos, jicama, yuzu, wasabi tobiko, jeijoa and kirmizi biber, and Turkish chilli flakes 'usually brought over from a friend in Turkey.' The waiting staff must spend a great deal of time explaining what the ingredients are.

SOURCING ALTERNATIVES

The alternatives to local food sourcing are supermarkets (for smaller restaurants), local wholesale and retail and cash-and-carry shops, specialist food companies and farmers' markets.

How not to source your food

There are several large, national wholesale suppliers such as Brakes, whose lorries criss-cross Britain and France. Their buying power is second to none and they dominate the market in chilled fresh and frozen food. I am sure you have seen their vans parked outside many restaurants, pubs, hospitals and other outlets.

Many in the hospitality business see this type of business as deskilling chefs, most of the products on offer being of the 'heat 'em up' variety rather than cooking from scratch. Their synthetic desserts, a particular bone of contention, crop up in many chain restaurants, as well as bland main courses, a travesty, in my view, of how restaurant kitchens should be run – with knowledge, understanding, hard work and quality in mind at all times. Resist going down this route if you want your restaurant to be respected.

The less we know about food, the less good, well sourced food will matter. Caring, responsible restaurants may therefore be fighting a losing battle to move sourcing to an altogether higher level of quality. Raymond Blanc once said: 'British chefs desperately need to sharpen up. They're not connected with their food. How can we encourage the UK to move from cheap food to "real food"? This applies to everyone's food, not just in the restaurant trade.'

The British Protected Food Names Scheme

The EU Protected Food Names Scheme (a British version of the *appellation controlée* system that exists in France to safeguard their wines) has been in operation for some years now. Cornish clotted cream and Jersey Royal potatoes are examples of the names it protects. The PFNS protects regional and traditional foods whose authenticity and origin are guaranteed by independent inspection.

Sourcing food from Britain

There are many organisations in the UK that promote local produce. One such is the New Forest Marque. Based in Hampshire, the organisation's ethos is to include only good local produce (such as goats' cheeses, crabs and lobsters, Dexter beef and other ingredients within the New Forest boundary) on its list. Unfortunately other organisations take all-comers, resulting in a mixed bag of produce, some of which is distinctly poor. When sourcing locally for your menu – whether it be via farmers' markets, local farms or smallholders and other sources – insist on quality because 'local' does not always mean this. Highlight on your menu where some of your produce comes from. Diners are keen to support local initiatives.

Obviously, however, not all produce can come from the UK. The best foie gras, black pudding, cured hams (like Parma), specialist cheeses, pistachios, limes, lentils and most wines are just a few of riches that come to our shores.

The Slow Food movement

Carlo Petrini founded the Slow Food movement in 1989 to safeguard Italian regional foods: 'A gastronome who isn't an environmentailist is a fool,' he declared, adding that 'people must know where food comes from and how it's produced.'

The Slow Food movement now has more than 100,000 members in 132 countries around the world, and it works to counteract fast food and the disappearance of local food traditions. It promotes sustainable agriculture as the foundation of an alternative and more beneficial food system. The Slow Food movement encourages people to identify themselves as co-producers, not consumers. Their remarkably strong ethos is that, by supporting food producers and understanding how we influence what is grown and sold, we become partners in the production process.

Website: www.slowfood.org.uk.

QUALITY AND PROVENANCE OF PRODUCE

We have a vested interest in helping farmers who look for alternatives to keep their farms afloat, but only if they can come up with the goods – the produce has to stand out. Since 1979, UK growers' produce has slowly dwindled. They now supply just 4 per cent of the fruit and 52 per cent of the vegetables we eat. Mangetouts from Peru travel 6,312 miles, green beans from southern Africa 5,979 miles.

Polytunnels

Polytunnels now produce up to 80 per cent of summer fruit. Five thousand acres of Herefordshire, Kent and Scotland alone are now pastures of plastic. The season has been extended by months thanks to this method of growing. Just down the road from me is Tangmere airfield, part of the Battle of Britain strategy and now one of Europe's largest pepper nurseries, with over 50 acres of glasshouses on its 115 acres of land.

Salads, herbs, vegetables, flowers and ingredients previously more likely to have been flown in from other parts of the world are now grown in polytunnels. The defence from growers is that 'it is British and good for the local economy', despite its desecration of the landscape.

The growth of polytunnels is largely due to supermarkets demanding reliable, unblemished fruit and vegetables. The former *Guardian* newspaper gardener, Monty Don, mounted a campaign with others against strawberries ('tasteless junk fruit') grown in 250 acres of 'ugly polytunnels' near his Herefordshire home. And he won. We should demand food that tastes of something rather than the current British strawberry, which is 'helped' along by 17 fungicides and 16 insecticides and still tastes of nothing.

USEFUL CONTACTS FOR SOURCING PRODUCE

Government agencies and other organisations are included in the following list, but there are plenty of other organisations and producers. Consult *Yellow Pages* and your local council and search the web.

A word of warning: just because it's local doesn't necessarily mean it's good. Be choosy! Locate the best produce possible and help to raise standards.

Chef suppliers directory (*Hotelkeeper & Caterer*): (0208) 62 4700 or email chotsen@rbi.co.uk

National and government agencies

National Association of Farmers' Markets: www.farmersmarkets.net

DEFRA (Department of Environment, Food and Rural Affairs): (0207) 238 6687 www.defra.gov.uk

Department of Agriculture and Rural Development (Northern Ireland): www.dardni.gov.uk

Regional

Buckinghamshire Food Group: (01296) 383345 env-edt@bucksscc.gov.uk

East Anglian Fine Foods: www.foodanddrinkforum.co.uk

East Midlands Fine Foods: www.eastmidlandsfinefood.co.uk

Food From Britain: www.foodfrombritain.com

Guild of Fine Food Retailers: wwwfinefoodworld.co.uk

Hampshire Fare: www.hampshirefare.co.uk

Heart of England Fine Foods: www.heff.co.uk

Henrietta Green's Food Lovers' Club: www.foodloversbritain.com

Highland and Islands Enterprise: www.scottishfoodanddrink.com

Kentish Fare: www.kentishfare.co.uk

New Forest Marque: www.newforestnpa.gov.uk

Local producers (www.buylocalfood.co.uk)

London Food Link: www.londonfoodlink.org

North West Fine Foods: www.nw-fine-foods.co.uk

Northumbria Larder: www.northumbria-larder.co.uk

Oxfordshire Food Group: (01865) 484116 localfood@brookes.ac.uk

South East Food Group Partnership: www.buylocalfood.co.uk

A Taste of Sussex at Sussex Enterprise: www.sussexenterprise.co.uk

Taste of the West: www.tasteofthewest.co.uk

Scottish Enterprise: www.scottishfoodanddrink.com

Scottish Food and Drink: (0141) 228 2409

Scottish Organic Producers Association: www.sopa.org.uk

A Taste of Ulster: (0289) 0665630

Tastes of Anglia: www.tastesofanglia.com

Wales: The True Taste: www.walesthetruetaste.com or 08457 775577

Welsh Development Agency: www.foodwales.co.uk

Welsh Organic Meat: www.cambrianorganics.com

Yorkshire Regional Food Group: www.yorkshireregionalfoodgroup.co.uk

Specialists

British Cheese Board: www.britishcheese.com

The British Herb Association: (0207) 331 7415

British Sheep Dairying Association: BSDA@btopenworld.com

The Chocolate Society: www.chocolate.co.uk

Culinary Events Ltd: events@thecheeseweb.com

Fairtrade Foundation: www.fairtrade.org.uk

The Garlic Information Centre: (01424) 892440

Specialist Cheesemakers Association: www.specialistcheesemakers.co.uk

Ethnic food companies and associations

There are many to choose from locally and nationally. Many supply via mail order.

Chinese and Asian Foods: Wing Yip: (0208) 450 0422

Japanese: Yaohan Oriental Shopping Centre: (0208) 200 0009

Indian ingredients: Patel Brothers: (0208) 672 2792

Italian ingredients: I Camisa and Son: (0207) 437 7610

Mexican ingredients: The Cool Chile Company: (0870) 902 1145

Moroccan ingredients: Le Maroc: (0208) 968 9783

Spanish ingredients: R Garcia and Sons: (0207) 221 6119

11

ORGANISING WINE AND OTHER DRINKS

Wine is one of the more misunderstood subjects for the would-be restaurateur. They need to know what to buy, how to buy it, how to price it and how to sell it.

This chapter deals with:

☐ wines;

☐ wine buying;

☐ storage;

☐ guidance for compiling a wine list;

☐ serving wine;

☐ how to deal with corked bottles; and

☐ wine and food and types of wine with food.

The diversity of wines is also discussed and a wine vocabulary list is included. Trading Standards' guidelines for alcoholic weights and measurements are also considered. Coffee, tea and water are also covered in this chapter.

GETTING WINES RIGHT

Jake Watkins, chef/proprietor of JSW in Petersfield, Hampshire has no fewer than 800 wines stored underneath his small bar floor, accessible only by a hatch. Yet his restaurant seats a mere 44. A highly knowledgeable and enthusiastic exponent of wine and food, Michelin star-holder Jake is perhaps an exception to the rule in the restaurant trade: he has both food and wine hats firmly on.

Your choice of wines is of great importance. To have a good, lengthy wine list, however, you must have enough storage space. You must also have the knowledge to source wines to match your menu. Obviously, if you're opening a small café with no licence, then wine is of little interest to you. Coffee is the all-important selling point. But for most restaurateurs it is vital to get the wines right.

Tips for buying and storing wine:

☐ Cellars are perfect for wine storage because they keep the wines at a constant cool temperature and the corks don't dry out. Wine doesn't like wildly fluctuating temperatures, vibration or warmth.

☐ Start with a small list because tying money up in wines can be costly.

☐ Seek the advice of a wine consultant or approach a wine writer if you are unsure about how to put a list together. Wine consultants and writers are generally freelance and are therefore subjective rather than tied to a particular supplier or producer.

☐ Are you to go for a safe, less than exciting list or are you going to take chances selling less well known wines?

☐ A good supplier will hold tastings for you and your staff. They will keep cases in storage for you, with the wines kept at the right temperature.

☐ A good supplier will go through the menu with you and marry wines with the food.

☐ The older wines become, the more carefully they need to be treated.

Don't have just one company to do your entire wine list.

THE DIVERSE WINE LIST

Gone are the days when French wine dominated the wine list. Wines from Australia, New Zealand, South Africa, Chile, Argentina, Spain, Italy and, to a lesser extent, the USA, Germany and Eastern Europe are now chosen as a result of the growth of wine retailing and, of course, of the vast improvements in wine making. Canada's British Columbia wines are a case in point. Don't dismiss other countries' wines just because they are unknown to you. The Lebanon, for example, has a long history of good wine-making.

Wine lists now match the diversity of the food on our menus. Previously unknown grapes, such as the spicy, fleshy viognier, the musky, aromatic pinot gris, the plummy voluptuous merlot and the rich shiraz, are now commonplace. Go beyond the Chardonnays and the thin Pinot Grigios of this world. These have dominated the market for far too long and are seen by some as an over-oaked cliché, unless you can source an outstanding ones.

Wines for the restaurant:

☐ Choose good house wines, not poor-quality ones.

☐ Not everyone likes chardonnay, especially over-oaked ones.

☐ Choose several house wines of differing grapes: sauvignon blanc, semillon, chenin blanc, viognier, cabernet sauvignon, shiraz, merlot, tempranillo and zinfandel are just a few to choose from.

☐ Most inexpensive and medium-priced wines are meant to be drunk immediately (i.e. not stored for future drinking).

☐ Have a good number of wines by the glass, not just two (one white, one red).

☐ Another popular way of selling wines is by the 50 centilitre or litre decanter. This gives a feeling of informality.

☐ Have a wide-ranging list, however small, and not just wines favoured by the restaurateur because these may not be broad enough for their customers' own tastes.

☐ Avoid well-known supermarket wines. Customers know their price and may be appalled by the mark-up.

☐ Don't palm the kitchen off with inferior wines to cook with. The poor quality will be noticed.

☐ Heading grape types with minimal information is a help for customers who may not understand the differing grape tastes.

☐ The cooler the climate, the leaner the wine. The alcohol percentage can be as low as 9–11 per cent.

☐ In hotter climates, wines will have tropical fruit flavours, many having a robust 14 per cent alcohol.

☐ Promote wines well, with information on the tables, by the bar and on the entrance menu.

Wine storage temperatures

Wine should be stored in a dark, secure, ventilation-free area that can be locked.

Red wine should be stored at 14–16° C and white wine at 10–12 °C.

Wording on the wine list

Keep the wording simple. Phrases and words such as 'excellent length' and 'cigar-box aromas' are best avoided. Vintages and premiers crus (first growths) are equally alienating for those customers with a shaky knowledge of wines.

You don't want to put your customers off buying a bottle, so make the wine list headings accessible. 'Wines under £12', 'wines under £20', 'light bodied', 'medium bodied' and 'full bodied' are instantly recognisable. For even greater simplicity, your wine list could have such headings as mellow, spicy, dry or sweet.

It helps sales considerably to keep not only the wording simple but also the headings. But entice the reader with your descriptions. Be concise and enthusiastic but avoid pomposity.

Wording such as 'aromas of blackberry fruit,' 'oaky earthiness' and 'ripe cherry fruit' can conjure up an instant picture but may also confuse your customers and highlight the restaurateur's poor understanding of wine, which won't inspire confidence.

If your restaurant is upmarket and your projected wine list includes vintages and big-name wines, you may wish to enlist the help of a wine writer or supplier. But still be as succinct as possible, particularly if the list is a long one.

There is no need to put the alcoholic content of each wine on the list, but this may be appreciated by those who prefer a less robust wine – or vice versa.

Tips for serving wine:

❏ Choose glasses that complement wine. Don't serve wine in Paris goblets because you barely have the chance to taste or smell the wine before swallowing it.

☐ Choose a plain, clear glass with a generously sized bowl that tapers slightly before the rim. The stem should be long enough for the glass to be held by the stem, not the bowl, as body warmth will heat up the wine.

☐ Clean glasses properly, making sure there is no washing-liquid residue on the rim because this will destroy the taste of any wine.

☐ Glasses need to be stored bowl up, not stem up, to stop them trapping stale air.

☐ Chill white wines, but not too much because this can dull their aroma and flavour.

☐ Red wines can be over-warmed in a warm restaurant, so take care where you store them (i.e. not near radiators, in a hot kitchen, in the bar by the coffee machine or by bright lights).

☐ There is no need to pull the cork on wines an hour ahead of drinking. The majority of wines these days don't really need opening up as they did in the past when reds were likely to be tough and tannic.

☐ Restaurateurs need to be able to talk with a degree of knowledge to customers about wine in general and their wine list in particular.

☐ Your staff should know about wine. Get them tasting. Make notes about each wine to give to your staff.

☐ When serving wine, your staff should always present the bottle to the customer before opening it.

☐ Train your staff to open a bottle properly by cutting the foil and removing the cork. Never try to extract a stubborn cork by placing the bottle between your knees and yanking it out.

☐ Train your staff to pour wine only half to two-thirds full in the glass so that your customers can enjoy the aroma, leaving room to swirl the wine around the glass.

☐ Customers increasingly like to be in control of their wine. The constant topping up by waiting staff in order to sell more wine is not acceptable. This is a hard-sell tactic that is not appreciated and the customer may not return.

☐ Always store wines on their sides, never upright.

Corked and other undrinkable wine:

☐ Corked wine: a musty, dank smell caused by cork contamination. Replace this.

☐ White wine with a sherry smell and usually with a dark yellow colour has been oxidised (too much air via the cork).

☐ A bad-egg or drain smell indicates too much sulphur in the wine.

☐ Thin, sharp wine may not be to everyone's taste, but if it's sour then it shouldn't be served.

☐ Stewed, baked, rather flabby red wine usually means over fermentation. This should not be served.

☐ Return all corked or tainted wine to your suppliers.

WINE AND FOOD

Traditionally, white wine went with fish, red wine with meat. In Britain today, however, there are no hard-and-fast rules. It may be argued that plainly cooked fish isn't suited to a robust tannic red, but serve it with a fruity light red and this is a successful marriage.

Most meals benefit from having a lighter wine first, then a fuller-bodied one; a drier wine before a sweeter one; and a younger wine before a vintage one. Raw, steamed and poached food is more suited to a light wine. Robust wines go better with roasts and chargrills.

Choosing wines to suit a whole table can be a problem. A wine that will go with the majority is the answer or suggest wines by the glass.

Dessert wines

Dessert wines are fast growing in popularity. Chill these well and serve them in small glasses. Once opened, dessert wines will keep for longer than other wines. Beyond the ubiquitous Muscat de Beaumes de Venise, the choice is sensational and good for your profit margins. Add several types of dessert wines by the glass to your dessert menu.

Types of wine with food

The following is a general guide but, as mentioned above, the rules are there to be broken:

Crisp, dry, fresh whites: salads, chicken and fish.

Smooth, medium-bodied whites: pasta, creamy sauces, chicken, salmon.

Full-bodied, rich whites: lobster, turbot, the slightly spicy style of Pacific Rim cooking.

Aromatic and medium-dry whites: Riesling with spicy Thai food, Gewurztraminer with Chinese, Tokay-Pinot Gris with foie gras.

Rosé: making a comeback. Good with sharply dressed salads and summer food.

Light, fruity reds: pasta, pizzas, chicken, vegetarian dishes.

Smooth, medium-bodied reds: almost anything. The French ones are more suited to classic French dishes.

Full-bodied reds: beef, game, casseroles and cold-weather food. An enthusiast's wine.

Champagne and sparkling wines: surprisingly versatile. A richer, fuller-flavoured champagne can be drunk throughout a meal, but try demi-sec champagne with fruit-based desserts because dry champagne with a rich dessert doesn't work too well.

Dessert wines: pure nectar. Muscats and sweet Bordeaux go well with apple, pear and peach desserts. Australian liqueur muscats partner chocolate with dash. Mavrodaphne of Patras, a red Greek dessert wine, matches chocolate too.

People go first of all for the price of the wine, then the country of origin and then the grape.

PRICING WINE

Customers take issue with the high mark-up on wines, especially if they recognise wine they can buy in their local supermarket or high-street wine merchant. The next thought that occurs to them is the wholesale price to the restaurant (i.e. the even lower price paid by the restaurateur). But, as wine merchant Alistair Gibson rightly states, retailers have to buy in wines and put them on their shelves. Their profit per bottle is around 28 per cent.

A restaurant offers an experience: waiting staff, glasses, the cleaning of those glasses, a chair, table, perhaps music. All of this has to be paid for on top of the rent, rates, insurance and all the other expenses that go with running a restaurant. There is also the money wrapped up in the stock and in keeping the wines in good condition.

Therefore, a profit of 60 per cent is the average for house wines. The other wines should be on a sliding profit scale. However, it is best to sell those wines rather than let them gather dust, so offer a 'specials board' of wines by the glass or bottle.

WINE VOCABULARY

AOC (*appellation d'origine controlée*): created by the French authorities to establish specific areas of production and grape varieties. It also covers maximum yield per hectare, sugar and alcohol, pruning of the vine, cultivation and wine-making methods.

Alcohol: an essential element in wine, alcohol is produced when enzymes created by yeasts change the sugar content of the grape juice into alcohol, carbon dioxide and heat.

Aroma: the wine's scent defined by the type of grape(s), fermentation and the age of the wine. The bouquet.

Barrel fermented: wine that is fermented in oak barrels rather than stainless steel tanks.

Blanc de blancs: literally 'white of whites', a white wine made with white grapes, like a champagne from chardonnay grapes.

Blanc de noirs: white wine made from black grapes.

Blending: also known as assemblage, the mixing of types of wine varieties to make a more balanced wine. Bordeaux wines are usually a blend of cabernet sauvignon, cabernet franc and merlot-fermented grapes.

Body: a wine with good tannic structure and good ageing potential.

Botrytis: a mould that attacks grapes either as grey rot (which may endanger the harvest) or as noble rot, which is used to make luscious dessert wines, such as Sauternes and the Hungarian Tokaji.

Claret: the British name for Bordeaux red wines.

Cru: literally, from the French, a 'growth'. It dates back to 1855, denoting a vineyard's rank in Bordeaux, which is then divided into five classes or crus.

Cuvée: literally, a 'vatful'.

Decanting: the separating of the wine's sediment. Decanting from the bottle to a glass container adds more oxygen to the wine to make it more palatable. If the wine is old, this can be a disaster because it can cause a quicker deterioration.

Fermentation, alcoholic: transformation of the sugar in the must into alcohol and carbon dioxide in the presence of yeast.

Fortified: a wine that has had spirit (brandy) added to it, like port or sherry.

Kabinett: high-quality German wines.

Must: unfermented grape juice obtained by crushing or pressing.

NV: non-vintage.

Oxidised wine: sherry-like or nutty flavour caused by the action of oxygen on wine due mainly to exposure to air, heat and light.

Reserve: for special cuvées (vats) set aside for ageing or for future use. This also refers to a minimum ageing period for certain spirits such as Calvados, Cognac or Armagnac.

Sec, secco, seco: dry in French, Italian and Portuguese, or Spanish.

Spatlese: late-harvested German wines.

Tannin: different types of tannins are created by the stalks, pips and skins from grapes, plus nuts, wood bark and berries, which are released during the fermentation process and the pressing. These tannins give the wine its specific character and contribute to its ageing. Wine storage in new wood allows extra tannins to be absorbed from the wood fibres into the wine.

Varietal: a wine made from a single grape variety. In France the wine must contain 100 per cent of the same variety, but in other countries small proportions of other varieties may be added.

Vintage: originally meaning the annual grape harvest. It now means a wine from the harvest of a particular year. Each vintage depends on a combination of climatic factors which determine the wine's quality and potential for ageing.

WATER, COFFEE AND TEA
Water

The consumer backlash against expensive, bottled water is gathering momentum, according to two studies recently in the *Guardian* which reveal that the UK's restaurant-goers overwhelmingly prefer to choose tap water over bottled.

The research revealed that tap water is the preferred choice for 63 per cent of people when they dine out. Yet despite this, one in four people surveyed said they have felt pressured to order bottled water when dining out.

More and more UK restaurants are offering tap water to diners as standard, which is already the norm in the USA, the *Guardian* continues. But you still often have to ask for it.

With profit margins of 500 per cent for most bottled water, it is not surprising that some waiters, as directed by their managers, are remarkably skilled at offering 'sparkling or still' as soon as a customer is seated.

Water pricing has become out of hand. Some diners are paying up to £4.50 for a litre of filtered tap water, which costs the princely sum of 10 pence. Or even a reported scandalous £2.50 per glass.

Coffee

In previous chapters I urged you either to hire or buy a good espresso machine to offer espresso, cappuccino, latte, americano and all the other types of coffee. Customers expect a good coffee after a meal, with a meal, before a meal or instead of a meal.

☐ Make sure your staff know how to operate your coffee machine. The company will help you with this, but don't lock yourself into a long contract with a machine supplier.

☐ Experiment with coffee, sourcing good suppliers.

☐ Grind your own beans for the best-tasting coffee.

☐ Have the right cups and saucers to show off your coffee. These may be obtained from the company that hires you the machine. Or you could buy appropriate cups and saucers. Dainty or 1970s squat, canteen-like cups are not suitable.

☐ If possible, go on coffee courses to understand the art of coffee.

☐ Market your coffee well.

Teas are increasing in popularity. Offer quality teas, including peppermint and other flavoured ones. Don't charge excessively for a teabag and some hot water if these hot drinks are offered after a meal. This could harm your business.

If you are running a tea room or café, on the other hand, you must charge accordingly. The space taken up by customers – and time – must be taken into account. At a recent visit to a reasonably smart London restaurant, two of us were charged £3.50 each for a peppermint tea bag dunked in hot water after a meal. No matter what the overheads are, this is unacceptable.

Other drinks

You will be stocking your bar or, in the absence of one, an area of your restaurant, with spirits, beers, liqueurs and soft drinks. Have the right types of glasses on adjacent shelving, and ice, lemon and other bar accoutrements, such as corkscrews, wine coolers and ice buckets, handy. Have cleaning materials to keep the bar clean and tidy, and tea towels for polishing glasses.

TRADING STANDARDS GUIDELINES FOR SELLING ALCOHOL

The pricing of all food and drink must be made clear to your customers. Have a price list. If you chalk your food and drink up on boards, make sure these are easily seen and are legible.

The price list should include:

☐ the price;

☐ the quantity (e.g. 25 ml of gin or $1/2$ pint of beer);

☐ the price for each quantity. If the price of a double whisky isn't the same as two singles, then show both prices; and

☐ VAT.

Display the price list

You must display the price list where food and drink are ordered. If the price list can't be read from here, you should display it at the entrance to the eating area. In restaurants, the price list should be displayed in the window or in the reception area so that customers can see the prices before they enter the restaurant.

Obviously, this is not practical for most restaurants, these guidelines perhaps applying to chain bars and restaurants. A drinks list is usually given to the customers with the menu, and this seems to suit restaurants and Trading Standards officers alike.

Weights and measures should, however, be strictly adhered to. Despite Europe being metric, Trading Standards are not totally metric:

☐ Beer, lager and cider, except when mixed with other drinks, can only be sold draught in these quantities:

– $1/3$ pint, $1/2$ pint or multiples of $1/2$ pint.

☐ Gin, whisky, rum and vodka: unless they are sold in cocktails, they may only be sold in these quantities:

– 25 ml, 35 ml or multiples of these quantities

– old imperial measures (gills) cannot be used for the sale of any spirits.

☐ A notice which is easy to read by customers must make it clear which quantity applies: in quantities of 25 ml or multiples thereof.

☐ The same quantity must apply in all the bars of pubs, restaurants or cafés.

☐ Optics or thimbles for measuring purposes must be stamped and where customers can see them being used.

☐ If you run out of a particular drink, you must remove it from the price list as soon as reasonably practicable.

☐ Wines by the glass must be sold in the following quantities:

– by the bottle

– by the glass in 125 ml, 175 ml or multiples of these quantities

– these quantities must be made clear to customers either in a notice or on every wine list or menu

– by the carafe in 250 ml, 500 ml or 1 litre quantities.

This is not an authoritative interpretation of the law and is intended for guidance only (courtesy of the West Sussex County Council). Contact your local council's Trading Standards officers for further information.

12

RUNNING YOUR RESTAURANT ON A DAY-TO-DAY BASIS

You have achieved your goal of owning a restaurant and it's time to open your doors to the paying public. You are staffed, the produce has been sourced and bought, you've had your opening party and the word is out on the street: *you are open.*

This chapter outlines some front-of-house essentials. It also outlines a small kitchen's daily work, which may help to set you on course.

Most restaurants have a daily pattern, no matter how many hours they are open, to deal with preparation, serving, clearing away and paperwork. Most start work from one to four hours before service, depending on the type of food served. If little of the food is actually prepared on the premises, then one hour will usually suffice but, if the food is cooked from scratch, the kitchen will be busy from early morning.

PLANNING

A well run restaurant has been planned in advance. If not, it will be chaotic and the business will suffer. First thing in the morning, the chefs will check the stocks (if they haven't done so and ordered the night before), making sure the menu's offerings can be covered adequately. Then the perishable goods are ordered and the dry goods checked and ordered if necessary.

PREPARATION

A menu comprising bought-in food will require less advance cooking, but salads and other garnishes may have to be prepped to enhance the food. A restaurant that serves food freshly cooked only can prepare some dishes. This is called the *mise en place* (literally, the putting into place) – preparing all the raw material as far as possible before assembling them when the order is received.

These preparations include soups, stocks, sauces, terrines, patés, boning and trimming meat and fish into portions and, increasingly, stews and daubes made with rabbit, chicken, beef, lamb and vegetarian ingredients. Vegetables, garnishes and other smaller kitchen tasks follow, as well as a break and a staff meal before the restaurant opens.

All this preparation is for speed of food delivery. Don't underestimate the time it takes!

DIVISION OF LABOUR

In small kitchens there may be only one chef, or a chef and commis chef. In larger ones the kitchen is divided into parties or sections for each part of the menu, which may include starters, sauces, meats, fish, grills, vegetables, salads, larder work and desserts.

When orders come through, each section will prepare its part, the final assembling of the food perhaps being done by the head chef, who will always check it before it leaves the kitchen. This is called 'the pass'. The food will also have its final check against the order to see if it matches before it is taken to the table by the waiting staff.

CLEARING UP

When the last orders begin to trickle through, this is the time when the clearing up begins in earnest, although keeping a tidy, hygienic and clean kitchen during service is absolutely vital. Items not used are labelled and stored away or thrown out.

If you are running an all-day and evening food service restaurant, the menu will be simpler. But all the steps – cleanliness, clearing up, keeping a tidy kitchen, a watch on perishables – must be adhered to.

Once the kitchen is back to its pristine state, the staff can be released for a break before the next session. Or the management might release the staff gradually, the first one to leave being the first one back on duty to start the evening's preparation.

FRONT OF HOUSE

Taking bookings

Your bookings book should be by the phone on the bar or in some accessible place. Each day should have a separate bookings sheet. Include a plan of the restaurant at the front of the book so that your staff can identify the table numbers. In restaurant-speak, the number of seats are referred to as 'covers'. Ensure there is enough space in the bookings book for the following:

☐ Time of booking.

☐ Number of people booked in.

☐ Table booked (if applicable) – a window table may be asked for.

☐ Contact telephone number (if people ask why, this is for several reasons: if a booking needs to be changed or cancelled for any reason, for example).

☐ Any requests (disabled/special diet/birthday surprise cake and Champagne).

 Spread your bookings. The restaurant that allows all its customers to arrive at 8.30 pm is courting disaster.

A good restaurant staggers the bookings for the sake of the kitchen and the smooth running of the business. But there will always be people who turn up late. This can create a log jam and they may have to wait in the bar, until a table becomes available. Explain this with tact. Offer them a menu and a drink (but not on the house unless the booking mistake was yours).

The booking sheet could also have a space for the name of the staff member who took the booking in case there are any queries.

Repeat the booking back to the customer to make doubly sure that the details are correct. If a customer turns up and you have no record of the booking or it has been recorded on the wrong day, you may have lost that customer for ever.

Finish the conversation with 'Thank you for your booking and we look forward to seeing you'. Little courtesies such as this will give your customers the confidence that yours is a caring, polite restaurant.

 **A good manager and staff know how to fill a restaurant. They know whether table ten is going to be free in two hours and if the people coming in are regulars who always like to sit at table ten. Regulars need that extra looking after – and to be addressed by their names.**

Your staff should be aware of people with communication difficulties. They should speak directly at the customer so that their face can be seen clearly. They should speak normally but more distinctly. Listening attentively to all customers is a good thing.

Welcoming customers

When customers come into your restaurant and the staff are all busy, the manager or another member of staff should at least smile and say 'I'll be right with you'. To ignore customers on entry will not win them over. They may leave.

Deal with one customer at a time. Give them your full attention and you will be appreciated. Attention to detail is one of the most important things to get right in the restaurant business.

Preparing for service

Check the booking diary for reservations. Allocate tables to customers (if applicable). Check the staff rota and the staff present. Go over the menu with your staff *before* and not during service. Waiting staff can make the difference between a good restaurant and a great one. Do they know what is in each dish and can they explain them to the customers? Check that your staff look the part and that they have washed their hands before they start work.

Menus

☐ Make sure the menus and wine/drinks lists are clean and complete. Discard any dirty or stained ones.

☐ Has the specials board been agreed with the chef and been written up clearly?

☐ See if there are any items not on the menu and make sure all your staff know what is 'off'.

Check the bar:

☐ Is the bar area tidy and functional?

☐ Are ice and lemon in place and the white wine bottles replaced in the chiller?

☐ Has the red wine been placed in the bins or racks?

☐ Is there a good stock of water, soft drinks and beer?

☐ Has the espresso/cappuccino machine been switched on and is pristine?

Housekeeping check:

☐ Has all the housekeeping been done satisfactorily (loo paper, clean loos, bins emptied, tables set properly, chairs wiped and dusted, any dead flowers thrown out and replaced by fresh ones)?

☐ Are the cleaning materials ready for wiping tables?

☐ Are the salt and pepper containers filled?

☐ If using trays for service, are these clean?

☐ Are the cutlery drawers filled?

Building up trust

If the kitchen is behind with the orders, the chef must inform the waiting staff so that they, in turn, can reassure the customer that they haven't been forgotten. Make sure your waiting staff introduce each dish to the customer, rather than just putting it down without so much as a glance. They should explain what the dish is. 'Braised shoulder of lamb with rosemary, potatoes and greens' is far better than 'lamb'.

Service

If the tables are set up for four, two, six, eight or any number, and if all places are not taken, the entire setting or settings must be removed.

The rules of service haven't changed much over the decades, with women being served first, and all food served from the left and removed from the right. No plates are cleared until everyone has finished eating. Clearing away must be done with the minimum of fuss and clatter. Once the main course has finished, salt, pepper, bread and butter must be cleared. This is noted and appreciated by customers.

There will always be something to clear. Your staff must be eagle-eyed and remove anything dirty to the kitchen or washing-up area. While tidying up after a busy service, good staff keep an eye on the customers, who may want another coffee, the bill or to ask a question.

Never be the kind of restaurant whose staff are eager to sell another bottle of wine but are never around when a customer wants to pay their bill.

The manager must be aware of all the tables. Is there one still waiting for a first course after half an hour? A good manager is aware of who is eating, how long they have been waiting and if there is a problem that needs solving.

After-lunchtime service

Repeat the whole housekeeping, bar, menu and staff process again. Include in this a check on the menu and specials board and for any changes for the next food service. The tables should be laid for the next service, the bar restocked and the menus checked for cleanliness.

The cash should be counted and reconciled with the bill totals and another float added to the system. This is particularly important after every meal service and after every changeover of staff, so that errors can be identified and discussed with the staff member in question.

If you have a restaurant which serves food throughout the day, the process needs to be continually updated.

During a lull, keep up with the paperwork, the bookkeeping, staff hours, invoices, letters of confirmation to a customer for a function and other necessities. Management and chefs may also be conducting staff interviews, which should be put in the diary for either mid-morning or mid-afternoon. Alternatively, all these duties may be taken over by management not involved in service.

Those new to the business may not wish to take a break during sessions. It will do you the world of good to get some fresh air, a change of scene, during that all-important lull between lunch and evening. This applies to all staff.

THE KITCHEN

Depending on the size and nature of the restaurant, the start of the day is a movable feast. As a restaurant chef/owner for a 28-cover restaurant I was responsible for the cooking, ordering, the *mise en place* and the organising of the staff. The restaurant was open from Tuesday lunch to Sunday lunch, and my then husband was in charge of front of house.

As someone once remarked, 'sleep is like rat poison. After a while you get immune to it'. Yes, you do. But an afternoon cat nap can do wonders.

A TYPICAL DAY AT SOANES RESTAURANT

I start my day at 8.30, ready for service at noon. I am aided and abetted by two in the kitchen, Mrs O who does just about everything else, and Jenny who plates desserts and doubles up as a waitress. She is joined by other waiting staff on weekends and busy nights.

The menu changes seasonally, with no specials board. I start on prepping stocks, soups, pastry and terrines, the items that require longer cooking and prepping. My menu consists usually of five starters, five mains and five desserts with an artisan cheese board. Time to check the deliveries which may start coming in anytime after 8.30 am.

Go through the order to see if it is complete and if the produce is of excellent quality. Return any produce that isn't acceptable with the van driver. If it's spotted later, call the supplier.

For more control there are ordering sheets, stock sheets, staff personnel information, kitchen equipment maintenance records, records of fridge temperatures and the *mise en place* sheets. In smaller kitchens, these steps may be less formal, particularly in one-man-band operations. In all kitchens, chefs have a notebook or, increasingly, a computer for recipes and ingredients and for when certain dishes were put on the menu. The head chef's management skills must be on a par with their cooking skills and menu development.

I either ask Mrs O to label and store deliveries or, if it is a slower day, I do it just to have a good check on freshness and stocks. Mrs O is also in charge of cleaning and may be sorting out the storage room, cleaning the restaurant or putting a pile of tea towels and kitchen whites on to wash. She is a gem and much loved and appreciated.

Start calling companies if deliveries are late (they could jeopardise lunch service) or if produce isn't up to scratch. Because my restaurant was in a small town in the country, deliveries from London came twice weekly only but local produce came daily if required.

Mid-morning: prep sauces, desserts and peripherals like dressings, making sure I have enough produce to cover an unexpectedly busy lunch period or devise other dishes to put on if I think the more popular dishes may all go.

If you are not very busy don't even think of the above step as it may result in wastage. Always, however, have some quick-to-prepare dishes up your sleeve with the produce in stock, should the need arise.

By late morning, lunchtime staff arrive, the rolls are baked, the butter put into dishes. Bookings are checked. All vegetables are now ready for both lunch and dinner service and stored away. We all sit down to lunch and a chat before service.

Lunch

Up the path come the first customers who are greeted in the conservatory and bar overlooking the South Downs. Drinks here first and orders taken or, if they are in a hurry, they go straight to the table and order.

Lunch is in full swing, orders being put on pegs in strict rotation. Vegetables are cooked to order in the Hobart steamer, the chargrill put to use for fish or calves' liver, a beurre blanc having its butter cubes whisked in, the salmon and tarragon terrine sliced and garnished, salads dressed just before being served, a chocolate pithiviers in the oven to be finished off and glazed then served with an almond sauce.

The swing door whisks open and shut between kitchen and restaurant. Laughter and the babble of voices come through to the kitchen where, surprisingly, there is little bumping into one another as we tend to anticipate our moves. Waiting staff know better than to get around the stoves anyway!

The cheeseboard is rescued from its chilly home (the law is an ass when it comes to being able to have cheeses at room temperature), five cheeses plated on to a rectangular dish with suitable breads and oat cakes in tow. The coffee machine hisses in the corner with yet another espresso emerging. Mine.

Service over

When service is over, the kitchen is left pristine. Staff leave for the afternoon, returning at 6 pm for a 7 pm start. I check the fridges for produce, make a list on the board of prepping to do and have a few hours off if it isn't a busy evening or a weekend.

At 6 pm the rolls go in to be finished off, bookings are checked, the stock pots strained, cleaned and put away to leave more room for a busy evening's cooking. When staff arrive, a meal is either eaten or, quite often, they eat off the menu after service at a high kitchen table and we go through the day and discuss anything that went wrong – or right! Or improvements that could be made, adjustments to the menu that might improve the sale of certain dishes and any feedback that emerges.

Showtime

But, before this meal, it is showtime! The orders come in, the plated food goes out garnished and followed by suitable vegetables, desserts plated and served. Chicken breasts spatter their skin fat on the range, steam rises from the mussels, the door between the pass flaps in and out.

That wonderful pressure is on to do 28 starters, main courses and desserts, the layering of the thought processes – which dish is cooked when – as complicated as attempting to play a game of tag with 28 people simultaneously.

Just four more orders to go. 'Please don't have the scallops with pea purée, I've only got one more portion!' They don't, going for the chargrilled lamb with a garlic sauce, roast sea bass with a sesame prawn crust, a wild mushroom risotto and beef fillet with Dauphinoise potatoes.

Shut down

Then suddenly the restaurant is empty apart from regular customers chewing the fat with front of house. The kitchen is scrubbed down, rubbish put out and staff check their rota after their meal.

At nearly midnight staff rev up their cars or motor bikes in the car park and leave, the South Downs beyond lit up by a flash of lightning. It is beautiful. And quiet again. But there is still the ordering to do on the phone, some more checking of produce and then the kitchen lights go out for another day.

WHY DO IT?

Why do people do it? It's a buzz. Being creative, giving pleasure, and working, learning and growing as a team. Trying out new ideas. Meeting an interesting crowd. It is mostly sheer fun, it's pure theatre, it's a living and it sure beats working in an office.

Of course it is very different in a large kitchen or in another type of restaurant. I only outline my experiences. Treble, quadruple the covers, the staff, the produce, the size of the organisation and it has to be even more scrupulously and meticulously worked out. And so well disciplined to work properly. Some see it as organised chaos. Some as a thing of beauty.

13
CUSTOMER RELATIONS AND BEING A CUSTOMER

When you run a restaurant, your responsibilities mainly concern your customers and staff. But what about the responsibilities customers have for restaurants? This chapter outlines both these types of responsibility and, with a foot in both camps, show you how to put yourself in your customers' shoes.

Handling customers is a skill you will acquire as your experience of running a business grows. It may be helpful, however, to have some pointers now to assist you on your way.

As hotelier and restaurateur, Kit Chapman (Castle Hotel and Brazz chain), in his *An Innkeeper's Diary* reports:

'Our clients are getting more demanding and difficult, not less. Attention to detail is the mantra we chant and success relies on our ability to respond to their wishes.'

'A carefully planned, well organised, perfectly well executed party is no guarantee of a satisfied customer. Any number of complex human ingredients may intervene: mood, prejudice, fear, personal taste, class snobbery, social inadequacy, megalomania, a row with the wife, the death of a pet.' (Take your pick.)

'We're in the mind-game – part psychology, part clairvoyance. We're in the business of making magic.'

Although a trifle depressing, this does demonstrate what the hospitality business is about and what can be achieved if you take on board the complexity of human nature.

CUSTOMER SATISFACTION

A good manager recognises that there has been a decline in customer satisfaction. The symptoms of this include the following:

☐ Increasing complaints about staff.

☐ Increasing complaints about the food or produce.

☐ More accidents taking place in restaurants due to poor maintenance.

☐ Arguments between staff which affect the atmosphere.

☐ Poor business morale.

☐ Breakages or shortages of equipment, resulting in staff being unable to do their job properly which, in turn, affects the customer.

☐ A high staff turnover.

Customers may also be aware of a lowering of standards by the staff:

☐ Do they smile at customers?

☐ Are they courteous towards customers?

☐ Do they say please, thank you, excuse me?

☐ Do they greet customers or congregate around the bar, ignoring them?

If this is the case, you should ask yourself if the staff member concerned is in the right job or has a problem that needs solving.

HANDLING COMPLAINTS

If a problem comes up and the customer makes a complaint, the following may help:

☐ Don't interrupt the customer.

☐ Never lose your temper.

☐ Don't take it personally (difficult, I know!).

☐ Don't argue.

☐ Don't put the blame on another person.

Do:

☐ Apologise for the complaint.

☐ Move to a quieter area with the customer if possible to discuss the complaint so as not to upset your other customers.

☐ Restate the complaint to show you understand the nature of the problem.

☐ Agree that the customer was right to bring that particular problem up (within reason, of course!).

☐ Act in a quiet, professional manner.

☐ Keep your voice low so that the customer's anger can be partly dispelled.

☐ If you feel their complaint was justified, offer to take the offending dish off the bill if this was the problem and to replace.

☐ If it was the service that was at fault, offer a glass of wine, a bottle of wine or free coffees all round.

PROMOTING CUSTOMER SATISFACTION

The following list highlights these factors that make for a good restaurant experience:

☐ The welcome, décor and ambience.

☐ The booking (if appropriate): has it been taken properly?

☐ The table's location.

☐ The menu and drinks list (content and cleanliness of the lists).

☐ The order being taken and identifying who the host is (if appropriate).

☐ The availability of the food on the menu.

☐ The speed and efficiency of the service.

☐ The pleasantness and courtesy of the staff.

☐ The staffs' unobtrusive waiting skills and attentiveness.

☐ The customer's ability to attract the attention of staff.

☐ Other customers' behaviour (e.g. rowdy, shouting, drunk, overuse of mobile phones).

☐ How complaints are handled.

☐ The method of presenting the bill and the collection of the payment.

☐ The departure and how this is handled (ignoring departing customers, being off-hand).

Putting yourself in your customers' shoes

Watch your staff to see if they welcome the customers. Discuss this with your staff if you notice any shortcomings. Sit at all your tables and look around you:

❑ Are the chairs comfortable and suitable for the type of operation you run? If you are sitting for any length of time over a meal, you don't want to squirm uncomfortably in your seat.

❑ Would you really want to sit next to a loo door, by a swinging kitchen door, by a draught from the front door or by coat hangers with coats brushing against your chair and maybe you?

❑ Are the tables big enough for bottles of wine, water, serving dishes, candles, flowers, cutlery, napkins, oversized plates? If not, decide what you are going to do about it.

❑ Are the tables clean and wiped down properly before a customer sits at one?

❑ Are the surroundings clean? Are those cobwebs and dirty marks you can see on the ceilings, walls and skirting boards?

❑ Why are these dirty, torn menus being given to your customers?

❑ Why are there streaks on the cutlery and the glasses?

❑ Why are these flowers past their sell-by date and not replaced?

❑ Why is the bar looking as if a bomb has hit it?

❑ Why haven't all those dirty glasses on the bar been moved to the washing-up area out of view of your customers?

❑ Have the staff washed their hands or has that waiter a dirty thumbnail?

❑ When serving the food, do your waiting staff tell the customers what the dishes are in some detail, and not just say 'fish, paté, soup, meat'?

❑ Why are the tables not being cleared properly and quickly?

❑ Why is a staff member's shirt hanging out and their shoes not cleaned and polished?

❑ Why are the windows dirty or smudged?

❑ What are your staff doing hanging out by the bins in full view of the restaurant and having a cigarette break?

❑ Why is the music so loud when you return to the restaurant after a break? Decide if this is the restaurant's policy or whether the staff are upping the volume while you or the manager are away.

☐ Why are the toilets not cleaned and well stocked with toilet paper, soap and paper towels? Analyse why this rota has not worked or put a rota in place.

☐ Why are there grubby marks on doors to the toilets, the kitchen and the entrance?

☐ If you can see inside the kitchen, why is it a mess? Why isn't it being cleaned properly?

☐ Why is food uncovered on a kitchen counter?

☐ Why are the bins overflowing?

☐ Why has this tired lettuce leaf been put on a plate as a garnish?

☐ Why are you eating a chicken breast that tastes of nothing or is of poor quality? Consider whether the chef is not ordering well and with care and if the cooking is up to scratch.

☐ Why is this stale bread being served to customers?

☐ Why is the wine not being chilled sufficiently?

☐ Why does this dish look as if it's been thrown on to the plate rather than prepared and plated with due care and attention?

☐ Why are people waiting for their drinks or food? Is there a hold-up in the kitchen? Or don't you have enough staff on duty?

☐ Why is the coffee from that very expensive coffee machine you so carefully found not being made or served properly? Consider whether your staff need more instruction on how to make good coffee.

☐ Are your staff working as a team? In the kitchen? In the restaurant? As a whole?

☐ How have your staff handled the bills and their payment?

☐ Do your staff say goodbye in a pleasant manner? Are they sullen or smiling?

This is a long list, but it is well worth taking the time and effort to go through it. If you find that some points needs attention, address them immediately.

BEING A CUSTOMER

Is the customer always right? No, of course not. While we may live in somewhat boorish times, with some unpleasant behaviour taking place in public spaces, there are many delightful human beings out there who will be charmed by your restaurant, your staff, your food and the ambience you have created. These are the people who will come to your restaurant, and you will be charmed by them.

Hopefully, they will remember to:

☐ Turn up in time for their booking and to respect your business, taking into account that your restaurant's system (i.e. putting pressure on the kitchen) might suffer if they are late.

☐ Call your restaurant if they are going to be late.

☐ Contact your restaurant if the numbers in their party are up or down as you simply can't magic chairs or tables out of thin air if the booking changes.

☐ Contact your restaurant to cancel a booking.

☐ Keep their drinking at a decent level and not get drunk on your premises.

☐ Complain politely if a problem occurs.

☐ Not treat your staff as servants but to see them as professionals and equals.

☐ Not complain over trivia.

☐ Say thank you for good food and service. This is music to your staff's, chef's and management's ears.

POSTSCRIPT

The following is a summary of an Edinburgh Festival mask show, 'Familie Floz':

'Ristorante Immortale is everywhere and nowhere. It is heaven and hell. It is the restaurant that never opens but never closes, has a staff that serves but never sleeps and it is where you can go eat your fill but still go back for more.'

'It is a metaphysical culinary Fawlty Towers where dreams and nightmares, comedy and pathos collide. It is like a waiter in a great restaurant eager to please and makes you feel like a valued customer.'

Should you decide to open a restaurant, I hope the information, experiences and practicality – aided and abetted by common sense – in this book have helped you on your way to an informed decision.

May you open and close when you wish, and may you have many valued customers who return for more and more of your rewarding hospitality.

I wish you good fortune.

GLOSSARY

STAFF

Chef de partie Literally 'head of a team'.

Commis chef The most junior chef, learning their trade.

Demi chef de partie Literally 'half' – fewer responsibilities.

Executive head chef In charge of a large restaurant or restaurants, hotel restaurants or a catering company.

Head chef In charge of the kitchen, staffing, menus and suppliers.

Kitchen brigade The name given to kitchen staff as a whole.

Kitchen porter The underpinning member of the kitchen who washes up, preps vegetables and is in charge of rubbish.

Sous (under) chef Head chef's immediate number two capable of carrying out head chef duties in absence of the head chef.

COOKING TERMS

Al dente An Italian term meaning 'to the tooth'. Cooking pasta with a resistance to the bite.

Bain-marie Deep pan of hot water in which dishes to be cooked are placed prior to being put in a low-temperature oven. Also a large water tray on top of the stove to keep sauces, such as Hollandaise and custard, warm without overcooking or spoiling them.

Bake blind Baking pastry cases without filling but lined with foil and ceramic or metal beans then baked prior to the filling being added.

Blanch/refresh Fast-boiling vegetables for a few minutes then refreshing them in cold water to keep their colour. A possible holding point for further cooking. Can also be for whitening meats or fish to remove any trace of impurities. Also for removing the skin from nuts, tomatoes, peaches and peppers.

Chambrer To bring cheeses to room temperature for maximum flavour.

Clarify butter Removing the milky residue by gently heating butter, then either pouring it through muslin or pouring it carefully into a container without disturbing the residue.

Confit Traditionally, confit only applies to lightly salted duck or goose cooked slowly in its own fat and then preserved in this fat. When ordered, the meat is then roasted. Nowadays it is widely misinterpreted on menus, sadly demonstrating the restaurateur's basic lack of knowledge.

Decant Pouring liquid – wine, meat juices, etc. – carefully from one container to another without disturbing the sediment.

Deglaze Adding liquid – stock or wine – to a pan in which meat has been roasted, then boiled to reduce, and whisked into the concentrated juices and crusty bits to form a gravy which is then strained and seasoned.

Gratin Food cooked in a shallow dish with a sauce and finished in the oven or under the grill to produce a crust thanks to the addition of breadcrumbs or cheese.

Julienne Cutting vegetables into strips or matchstick shapes.

Jus Very often misinterpreted, 'jus' is short for 'jus de viande' (juices of the meat). Nowadays it is a sauce halfway between a gravy and a complex sauce made from stock, wine and other seasonings.

Lardons Small strips of bacon, salt pork or pork fat blanched then sautéed.

Monter Whisking cold cubes of butter into a sauce to thicken it. Can also mean whisking egg whites lightly or stiffly.

Reduce Reducing a stock or sauce by evaporation over a high heat until it reaches the wished-for consistency. This intensifies the flavours.

Relax Relaxing meat after cooking allows the re-balancing of juices and enhances the colour of red meat.

Roux A mix of fat (usually butter) and flour which is whisked in little by little to thicken a sauce. It must be cooked for quite a while to eliminate the taste of raw flour.

Sautéing Literally 'to jump' (French). The shallow frying of smallish pieces of food in an open pan with fat to brown them.

Supreme The skinless breast and wing of chicken or game, such as pheasant. Can also be applied to fish fillets to glamorise them on menus.

Sweat Cooking food over a gentle heat, usually in oil and/or butter, until softened but without colour.

Terrine An ovenproof, usually loaf-shaped dish for cooking patés with or without a pastry crust.

Tournedos A small, round, usually expensive steak cut from the thickest part of the fillet. Trimmed of all sinew and fat.

Tourner or **to turn** Cutting vegetables into olive, almond or barrel shapes.

Wilt Usually a green leaf or herb with a few drops of water from its washing, turned with tongs in a hot pan until just wilted but retaining its colour.

MISCELLANEOUS

Corked wine Wine that has been tainted by a contaminated cork.

Mirin Japanese sweet cooking wine made from fermented yeast rice grains.

Miso A savoury paste of cooked soya beans with grains, yeasted grains and sea salt which is fermented for one or two years.

Quinoa (pronounced 'keen-wha') Gluten-free grain similar to bulgar wheat used instead of rice, couscous or bulgar for those on a gluten-free diet.

USEFUL CONTACTS

British Chambers of Commerce **www.britishchambers.org.uk**

British Hospitality Association **www.bha-online.org.uk** (020) 7404 7744

British Institute of Innkeeping **www.bii.org** (01276) 684449

Business Debtline (0800) 197 6026

Business Eye in Wales **www.businessconnect.org.uk** (08457) 9697 98

Business Gateway (Scotland-Lowlands) **www.bgateway.com** (0845) 609 6611

Business Link **www.businesslink.gov.uk** (0845) 600 9006

Companies House **www.companies-house.gov.uk** (0870) 333 3636

Equal Opportunities Commission **www.eoc.org.uk** (0845) 601 5901

Federation of Small Businesses **www.fsb.org.uk**

Food Standards Agency for an A–Z of whom to contact (from alcoholic drinks to waste issues) (020) 7276 8000

Food Standards Agency for publications **www.food.gov.uk** (0845) 606 0667

Food Standards Agency website for caterers **www.food.gov.uk/cleanup**

Health and Safety Executive **www.hse.gov.uk** (08701) 545500

Henrietta Green's Food Lovers' Fairs **www.foodloversfairs.com**

HM Customs & Excise National Advice Service (0845) 010 9000

Highlands and Islands Enterprise (Scotland-Highlands) **www.hie.co.uk**

Home Office helpline on overseas workers **www.ind.homeoffice.gov.uk** (0845) 010 6677

Imported Food Helpline (020) 7276 8018 (Food Standards Agency)

Inland Revenue **www.inlandrevenue.gov.uk**

Landlord disputes **www.bdl.org.uk**

National Association of Farmers' Markets **www.farmersmarkets.net**

National Minimum Wage helpline (0845) 600 0678

New Employers' helpline (0845) 607 0143

Papworth Trust **www.papworth.org.uk**

Part-time workers' regulations **www.dti.gov.uk/er/ptime.htm**

Performing Rights Society **www.prs.co.uk**

Rare Breeds Survival Trust **www.rare-breeds.com**

Restaurant Association **www.ragb.co.uk** (020) 7831 8727

Small Business Service **www.business.link.gov.uk**

VAT helpline (0845) 010 9000

WI Markets **www.wimarkets.co.uk**

See Chapter 10 for further contacts.

BIBLIOGRAPHY

Small Business Co. UK; The Restaurant Association of Great Britain; *Caterer and Hotelkeeper*; www.foodreference.com; www.datamonitor.com; *Eating British*; *British Cheese Directory*; *The British Regional Food and Drink Guide*; *Observer*; *Observer Food Magazine*; *Evening Standard*; *Guardian*; *The Times*; Food Standards Agency; Performing Rights Society; Papworth Trust; Home Office; Inland Revenue; HM Custom & Excise; Immigration Service; Department of Trade and Industry; *In Business* (BBC Radio Four); *Yellow Pages*; Federation of Small Businesses; British Chamber of Commerce; Walnut Tree Inn, Monmouthshire; Brake Catering.

Beckett, Fiona *Wine by Style* (1998) Mitchell Beazley.

Chapman, Kit *An Innkeeper's Diary* (1999) Weidenfeld & Nicholson.

Erdosh, George *Start and Run a Catering Business* (2001) Self-counsel.

Gray, Rose, Rogers, Ruth *River Café Cook Book Green* (2000) Ebury Press.

Grigson, Sophie *Sophie Grigson's Herbs* (1999) BBC.

Hughes, Diana and Golzen, Godfrey *Running your own Restaurant* (1986) Kogan Page.

Johnson-Bell, Linda *Good Food Fine Wine* (1999) Cassell.

Ladenis, Nico *My Gastronomy* (1987) Ebury Press.

Lehrian, Paul *The Restaurant* (1953) Practical Press.

Lillicrap, Dennis, Cousins, John, Smith, Robert *Food and Beverage Service* (1998) Hodder & Stoughton.

Little, Alastair *Keep It Simple* (1993) Conran Octopus.

McKenna, John *How to run a Restaurant* (1998) Estragon Press.

Parker, Ken *Buying and Running a Small Hotel* (1992) How To Books.

Parkinson, Andrew, Green, Jonathan *Cutting It Fine* (2001) Jonathan Cape.

Riley, Michael *Managing People* (2000) Butterworth Heinemann.

Roux, Albert, Roux, Michel *New Classic Cuisine* (1983) Macdonald.

Weller, Lyn *Health and Vitality Cookbook* (2000) HarperCollins.

Whyte, Stewart *Starting and Running a B & B* (2003) How To Books.

Wood, Martin *Leith's Guide to setting up a Restaurant* (1990) Merehurst.

INDEX

a la carte menu, 145

AA Guide top ten tips, 142

AA Restaurant Guide, 96

accident, notification of, 22

advertising, 86 – 9

advertising wording, 88 – 9

advertorials, 88

agencies, recruitment, 111 – 12

alcohol licences, 20

alcohol, selling, trading standards guidelines, 170 – 1

alcohol, weights and measures, 171

Alice Waters, 138

allergies, 147

alternative sourcing, 154

Andrew Pern, 154

appearance, staff, 126

audience, targetting, 86 – 7

balance, menu, 139 – 40

bar and hall, 61

bar, 177

bookings, spreading the, 175

bookings, taking, 175

bookkeeping and accountancy, 41

bottled water, 169

brakes, 154

Britain, sourcing food from, 155

British Chamber of Commerce, 49

British Protected Food Names Scheme, 155

brochures, 84

business advice organisations, 48

business cards, 84

business debtline, 48

business partners/investors, raising capital and obtaining, 37

business plan, a, 29

business, expanding your, 100 – 7

business, financing your, 28 – 32

business, franchising a, 14

business, local government and your, 14

business, marketing your, 80 – 107

capital expenditure, 38 – 40

career, kitchen, 125

catering, outside, 103

ceilings, walls and flooring, 64

chairs, 63

champagne, 166

Chapman, Kit, 28

charges, extra, 34

chef de partie, 124

chef, commis, 124

chef, head, 125

chef, sous, 124

chefs, women, 126

china and tableware, buying, 75 – 6

classes, cookery, 101

classes, types of, 102

cleaning tips, 132 – 3

coffee machine, 169

coffee, water, tea, 169 – 70

column or cookbook, writing a, 106

comment and loyalty cards, 100

commis chef, 124

company, forming a, 30

complaints, handling, 184

contamination, avoiding, 52 – 5

Conran, Sir Terence, 153

cookbook or column, writing a, 106

cookery classes, 101

cooking terms, 190 – 1

corked wine, 165

corporate lunches, 105

costs, working out the, 31

cover charges, 34

creating income, 28

credit cards, 47

critics, approaching, 94 – 5

critics, dealing with, 93 – 4

culinary checklist for choosing chefs, 114 – 15

cultural and religious dietary requirements, 148

current trends, spotting, 10

customer relations, 183

customer satisfaction, 183 – 4

customer satisfaction, promoting, 185 – 7

customer, being a, 188

customers, creating contented, 140
customers, welcoming, 176
cutlery, 67, 77, 78

day to day basis of running your restaurant, 173 – 82
demi chef de partie, 124
design and equipment, choosing, 59 – 79
design, professional, 59
designing menus, 134 – 50
designing your restaurant, 59 – 60
dessert wines, 165
diabetic diet, 147
disabled access and facilities, 23
discrimination, 25
dish creation, 138
DIY design, 60
dress code, behaviour and communicating with customers, 126 – 30
drinks, other, 170
drugs, 127

employing foreign nationals, 121 – 2
employing people, 118 – 33
employment interview, 115 – 16
Employment Rights Act 2002, 120 – 1
employment tips, 116 – 18
environmental health office, role of, 56 – 8
environmental health, 55 – 8
equipment and design, choosing, 59 – 79
equipment, buying 71 – 5
equipment, kitchen 70 – 1
ethnic food companies and associations, 159
executive head chef, 190
expenditure, capital, 38 – 40

finance, attracting, 36
financial base, developing a, 28
finding staff, 110 – 12
fire certification, 22
first-rate produce, using, 137
flooring, walls and ceilings, 64
flowers, 67
flyers, 84
food and wine, 165
food consistency, 134
food poisoning, 52 – 5
food poisoning, preventing, 54
food poisoning, types of, 52 – 5

Food Premises Regulations, 50 – 1
Food Safety Regulations, 50 – 1
food storage, 51 – 2
Food Writers, Guild of, 106
food, garnishing your, 136
food, types of wine with, 166
franchising a business, 14
fraud and theft, 46
front of house, 175
functional restaurant, 60 – 1

garnishing your food, 136
glasses, 67 – 8
glossary, 190 – 2
Good Food Guide, 97, 153
Guardian Media Guide, 106
guides, restaurant, 95 – 6
Guild of Food Writers, 106

Harden's UK Restaurants, 97 – 8
head chef, 125, 190
health, environmental, 55 – 8
Hotel Proprietors' Act, 25
housekeeping checks, 177
hygiene, 127
hygiene facilities, 17
hygiene, staff, 55

importance of service, 109 – 10
insurance, 44 – 6
Internet, the, 85

Jake Watkins, 160
Jameson Guide, 97
JSW restaurant, Petersfield, 160

Kit Chapman, 183
kitchen brigade, 190
kitchen career, 125
kitchen equipment, 70
kitchen flow, 70
kitchen hierarchy terminology, 123 – 5
kitchen layout, 15
kitchen legislation, 70
kitchen needs, 69
kitchen porter, 124,
kitchen staff, 110
kitchen, laying out the, 68 – 9

knives, 75
KP, 124, 190

leasehold or freehold, buying, 12
leases, a brief guide, 13
legal tips, 47 – 8
legislation, kitchen, 70
licences, 20
licences, personal, 21
licences, public entertainment, 21
lighting, 65 – 6
local producers, 159
locally, sourcing, 152 – 4
location, design and legal requirements, 8
location, location, location, 9
low cholesterol diet, 147
low salt diet, 147
loyalty and comment cards, 100
lunches, corporate, 105

management skills, 130
market, target, finding your, 81
marketing tips, 89
marketing your business, 80 – 107
material, promotional, 83 – 6
maternity rights, 122
meals, staff, 123
media coverage, how to achieve, 90 – 1
media profile, creating your, 90 – 3
media research, 91
meeting and greeting, staff, 127 – 8
menu and drink pricing, 140
menu balance, 139 – 40
menu costings and prices, calculating, 31
menu planning and dish creation, 138
menu supplement charges, 34
menu, a la carte, 145
menu, creating a, 135 – 6
Menu, table d'hote, 145
menu, the importance of, 134
menu, writing and compiling, 142 – 7
menus, 85, 176
menus, designing, 134 – 50
menus, tips for, 145 – 7
menus, types of, 143
Michelin Guide, 98 – 9
Mise en place, 173, 179
money, raising the, 37
motivate people, how to, 113

motivating your staff, 112 – 13
music, 22, 127

name, choosing your restaurant's, 81 – 2
national and government agencies, 157
national minimum wage, 119
newsletters, 84 – 5
Nico Ladenis, 135 – 6

outside catering, 103
overtime, staff, 118

partnership, working in a, 38
part-time workers' regulations, 121
pay regulations and working time, 120 – 1
payroll, 44
personal licences, 21
pest control, 19
Peter Gordon, 154
planning, menu, 138
poisoning, food, preventing, 54
polytunnels, 156
premises licences, 21
press releases, 92 – 3
price list, displaying, 171
price marking, 26
pricing, menu and drink, 140
produce, using first-rate, 137
professional waiting skill tips, 129
promotional material, 83 – 6
property ladder, taking the first steps, 11
property, scrutinising a, 15
provenance and quality of produce, 156
providores, 154
public entertainment licences, 21
publicity, 84 – 6

Race Relations' Act, 25
recipes, following, 148 – 50
recruitment agencies, 111 – 12
recruitment, sources of, 111 – 12
redundancy payment, 122
reference, staff, 117
refuse storage, 18
regional food groups, 157
releases, press, 92 – 3
renting the property, 12
restaurant, decidiing what kind of, 5
restaurant, designing your, 59 – 60

restaurant, staffing a, 108 – 33
restaurant's name, choosing your, 81 – 2
restaurants, new trends in, 6
restaurateur, seeing yourself as a, 3
reviews, responding to, 94
rotas, staff, 131 – 2

safe business, running a, 50 – 1
Sale of Goods and Trade Description Acts, 24
school age, compulsory, 120
service charges, 34, 35
service charges, voluntary, 35
service, 177
service, importance of, 109 – 10
service, organising the, 78
service, staff, 128
Sex Discrimination Act, 25
sexes, menu war of the, 135
signage, 82 – 3
sinks and washing up equipment, 17
skills, management, 130
slow food, 155 – 6
Small Business Service, 49
Small Businesses, Federation of, 48
smoking, 22, 127
Soanes restaurant, 152, 179
sourcing alternatives, 154
sourcing locally, 152 – 4
Sous chef, 124
special diets, 147 – 8
specialists (food), 158
staff hygiene, 55
staff meals, 123
staff references, 117
staff rotas, 131 – 2
staff, 190
staff, finding, 110 – 12
staff, front of house, 109
staff, kitchen, 110
staff, motivating your, 112 – 13
staff, unskilled, 112
staff, waiting, 109
staffing a restaurant, 108 – 33
Star Inn, Harome, 154
stationery, 84
suppliers, choosing, 151 – 9
suppliers, key, looking for, 151
suppliers, working with your, 151 – 2

table d'hote menu, 145
table linen, 66
table, dressing a, 66
tables, 62
tap water, 169
target market, finding your, 81
tea, coffee, water, 169 – 70
team working, 126
teas, 170
temperatures, wine storage, 163
temporary and occasional events' licences, 21
theft and fraud, 46
Time Out, 99 – 100
tipping, 36
tips, legal, 47 – 8
toilets, 64 – 5
trade union membership, 123
trading standards guidelines for selling alcohol,
    170 – 1

underplates, 76
unfair dismissal, 122
unskilled staff, 112

VAT, 42
VAT, accounting, 42
VAT, registering for, 42
ventilation requirements, 16
vocabulary, wine, 167 – 9

waiting skill tips, professional, 129
waiting staff, 109
walls, flooring and ceilings, 64
water supply and drainage, 17
water, bottled, 169
water, coffee, tea, 169 – 70
water, tap, 169
weights and measures, alcohol, 171
welcoming customers, 176
wine and food, 165
wine and other drinks, organising, 160 – 73
wine list, diverse, 161 – 2
wine list, wording on the, 163 – 5
wine pricing, 167
wine storage temperatures, 163
wine vocabulary, 167 – 9
wines, dessert, 165
wines, getting wines right, 160

women chefs, 126
working time and pay regulations, 120 – 1
Writers' Handbook, The, 106
writing a column or cookbook, 106

Zagat Survey, 100